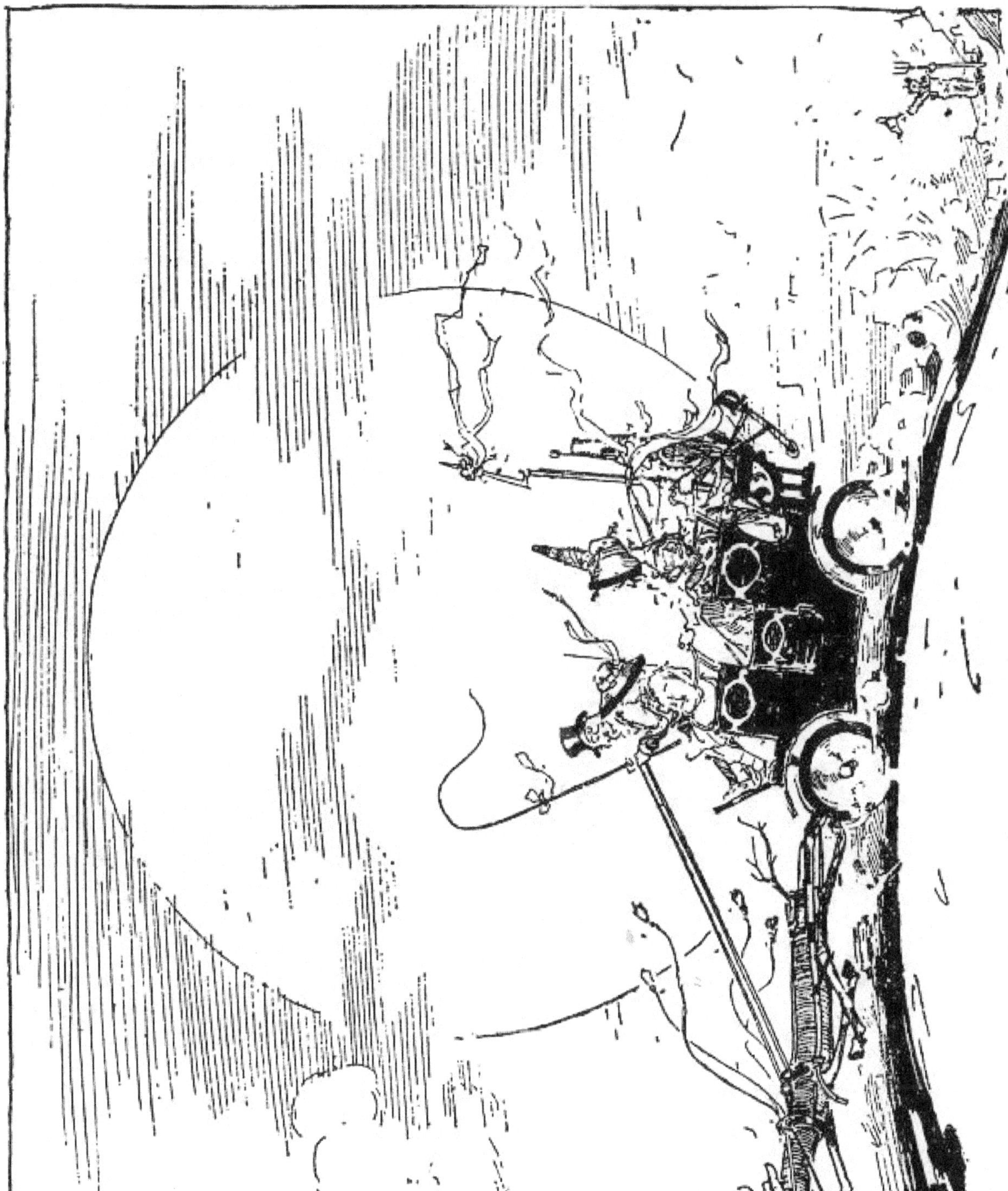

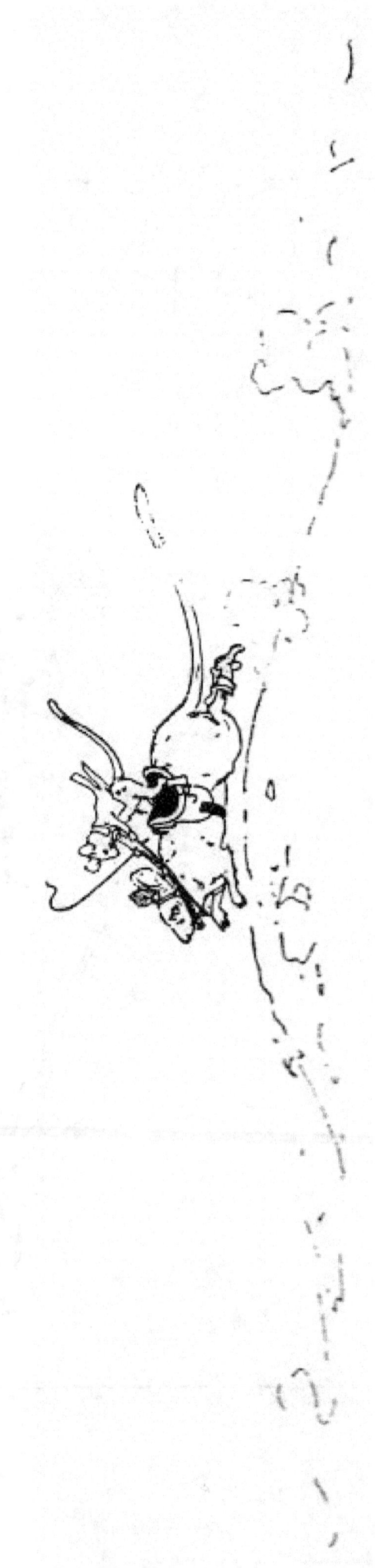

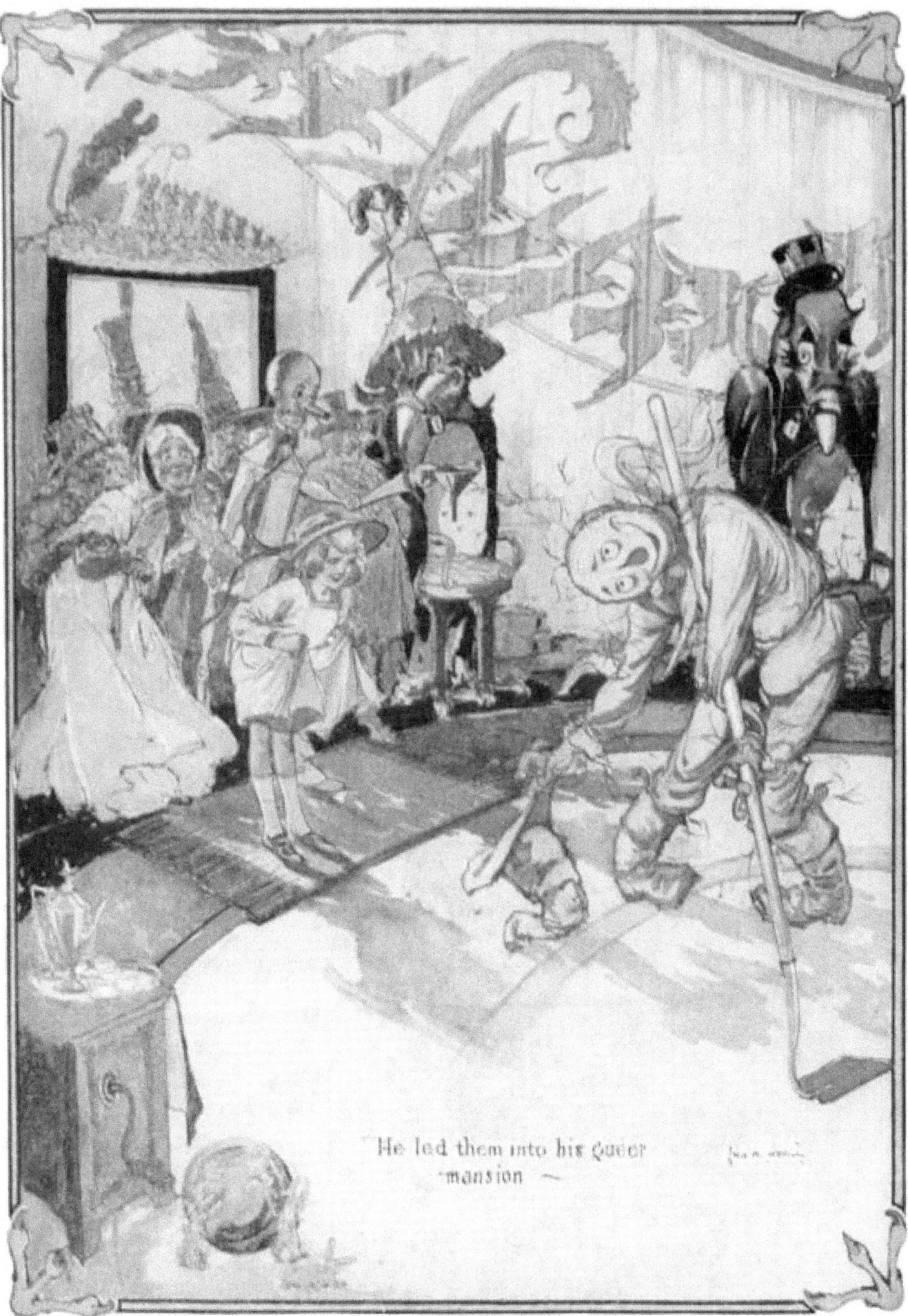

He led them into his queer
mansion —

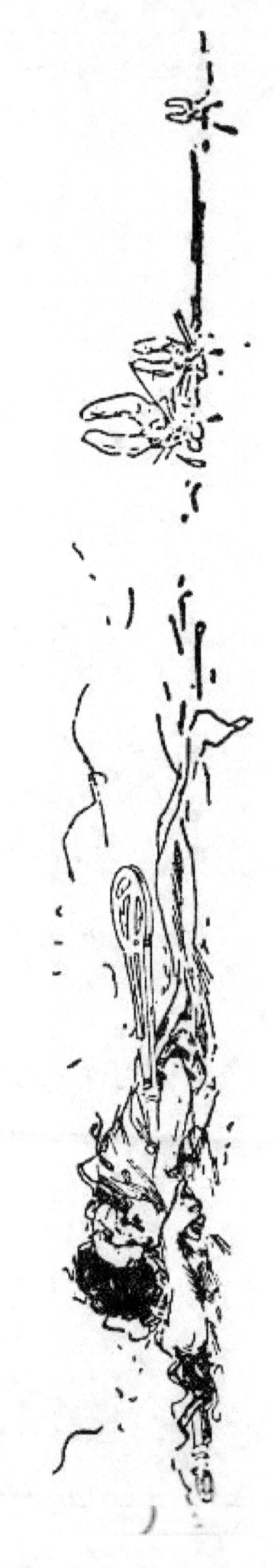

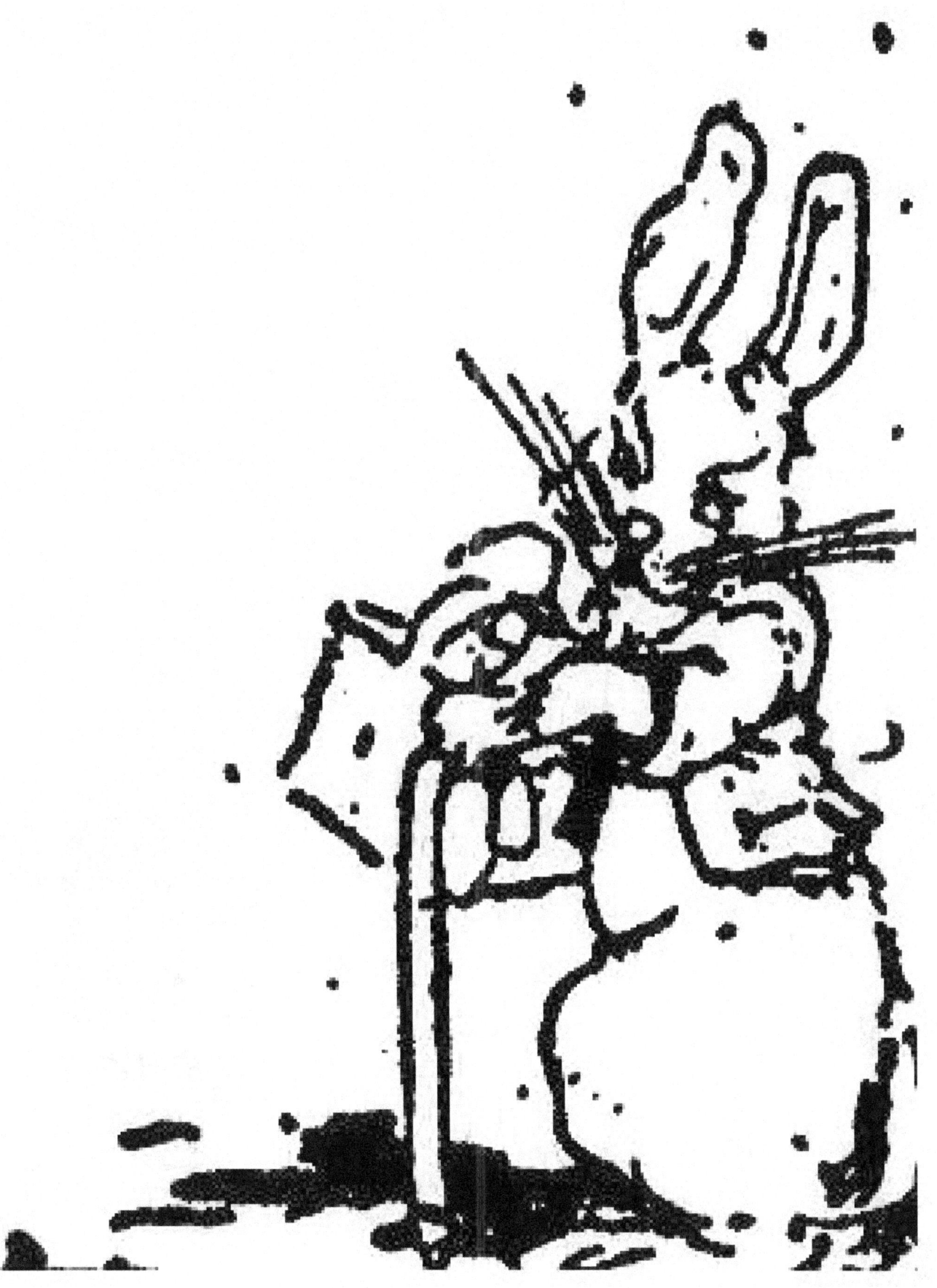

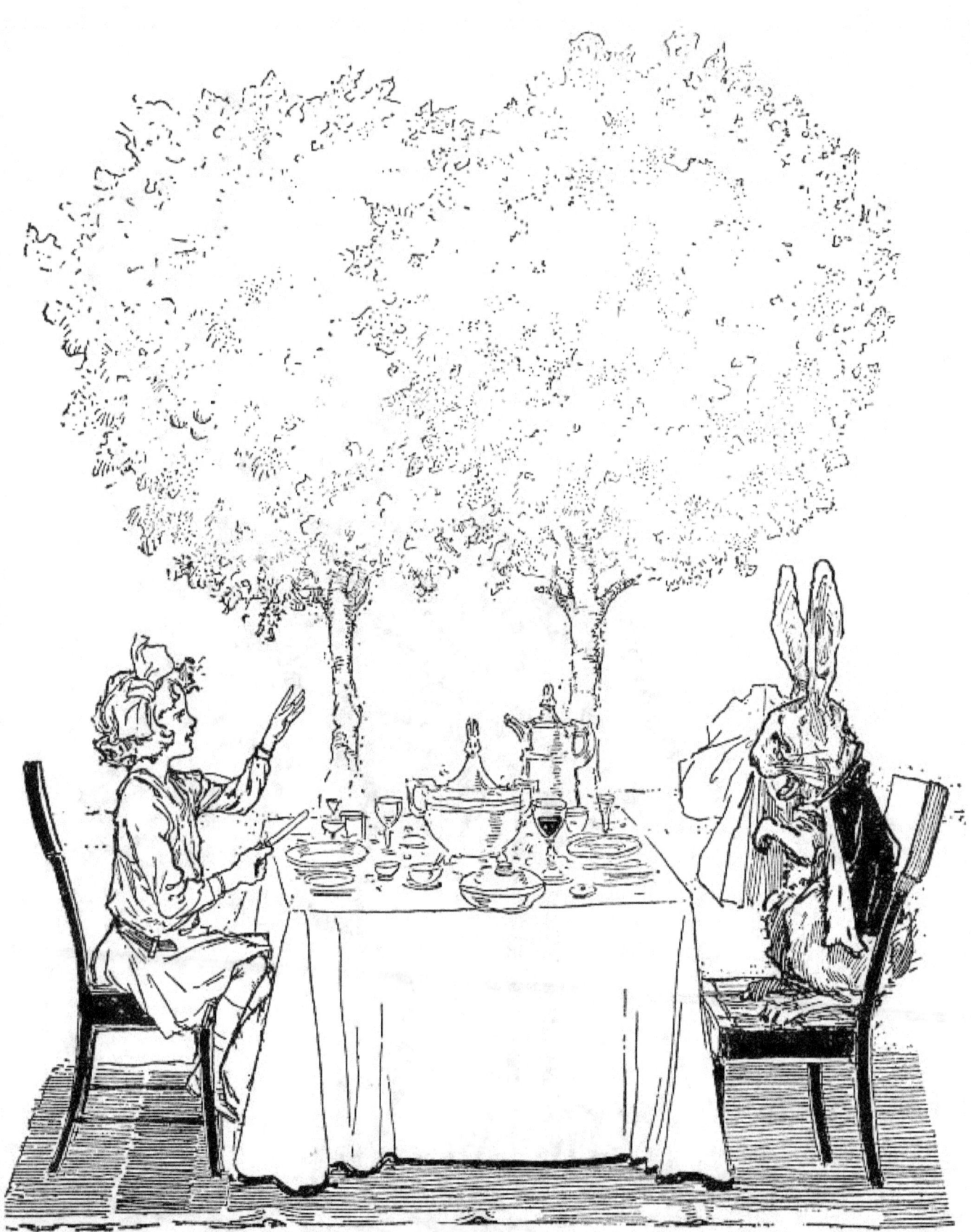

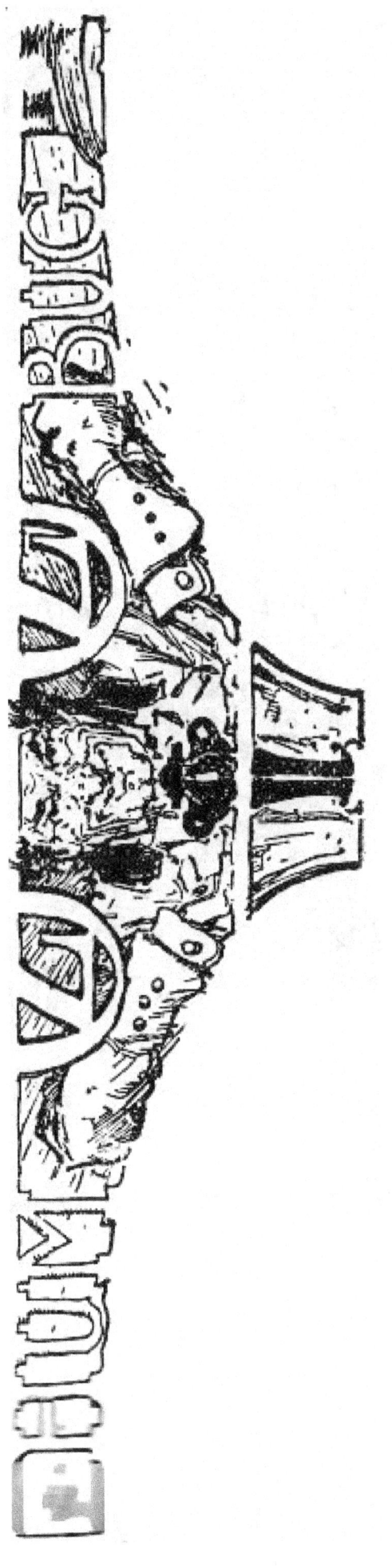

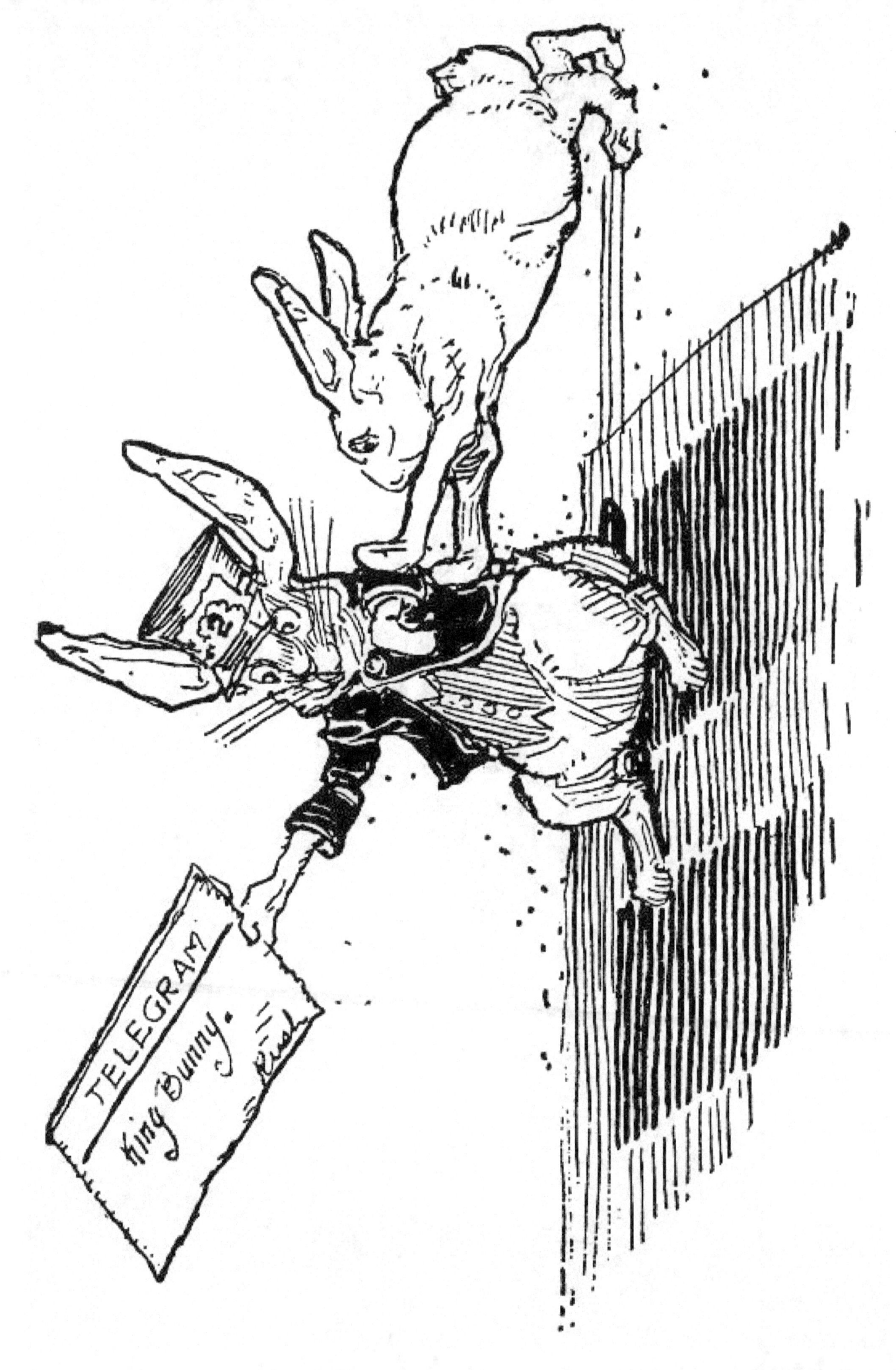

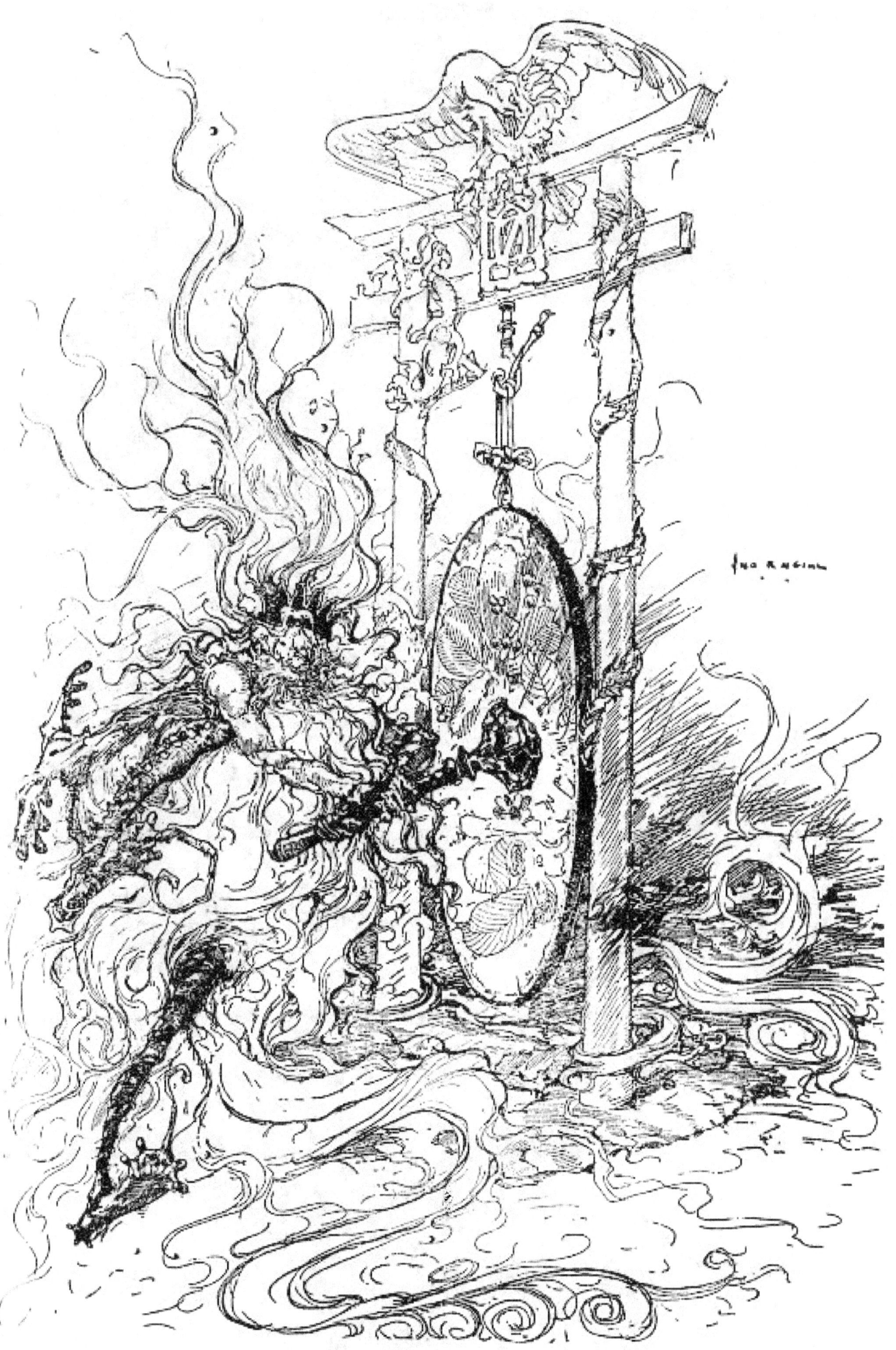

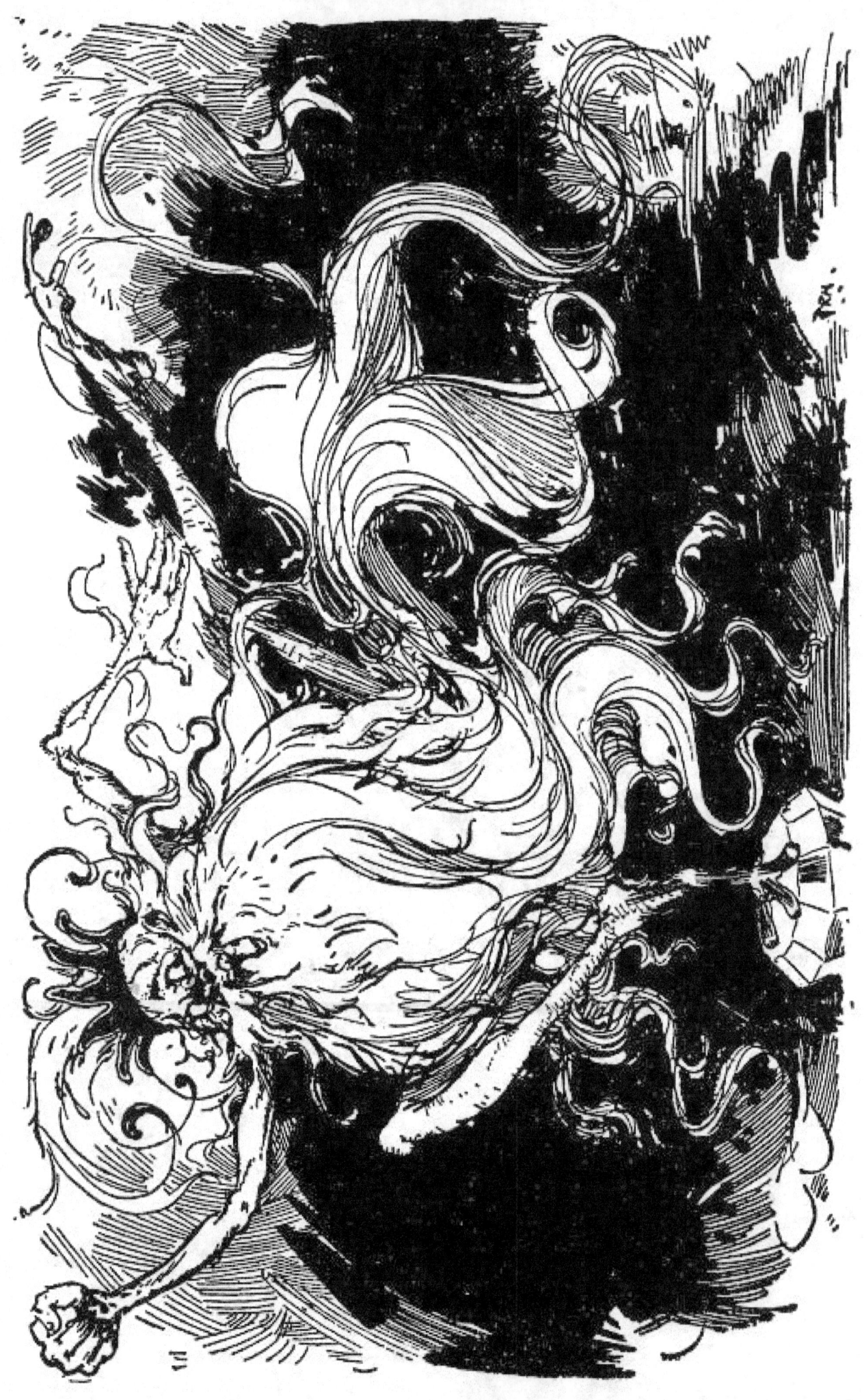

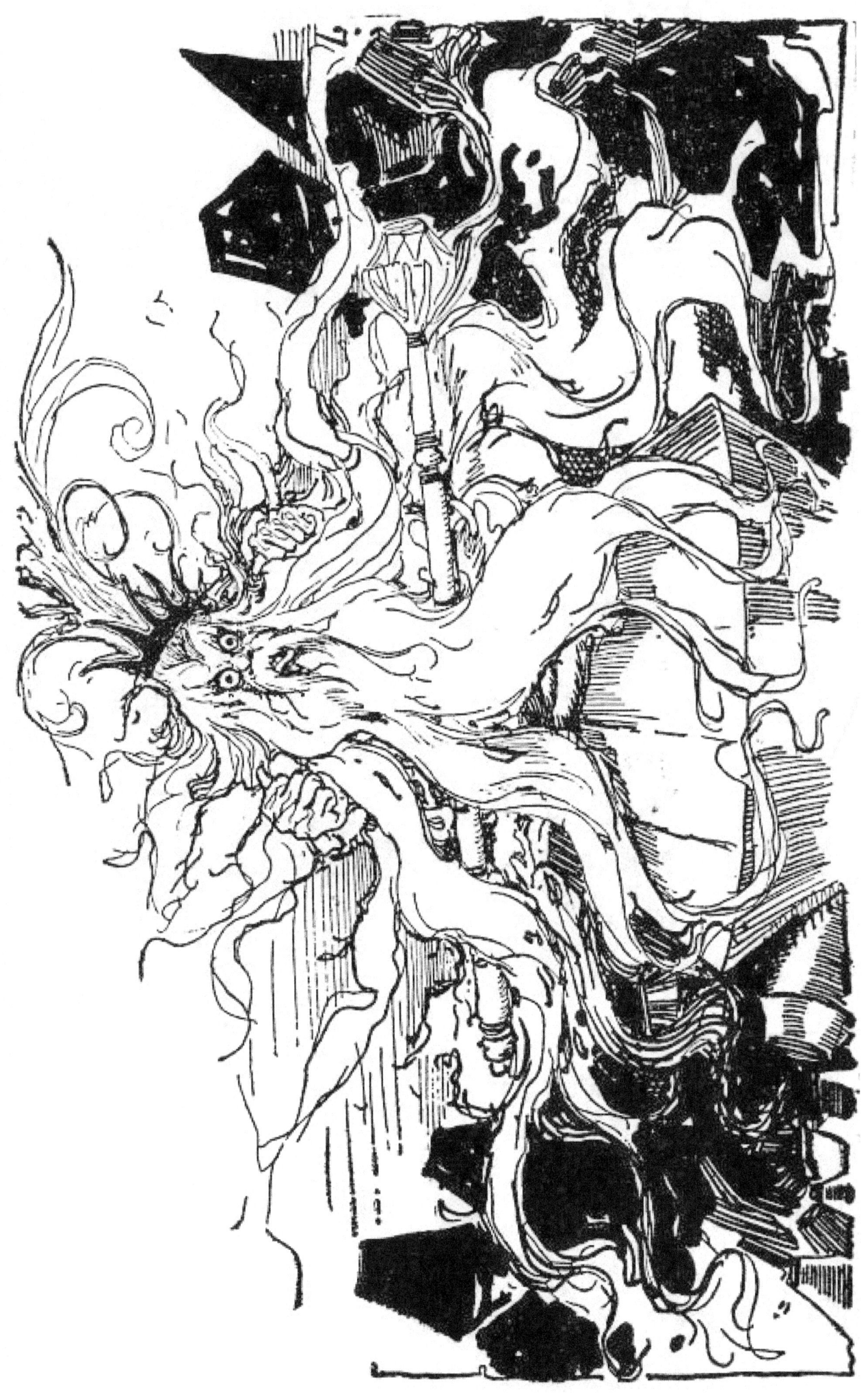

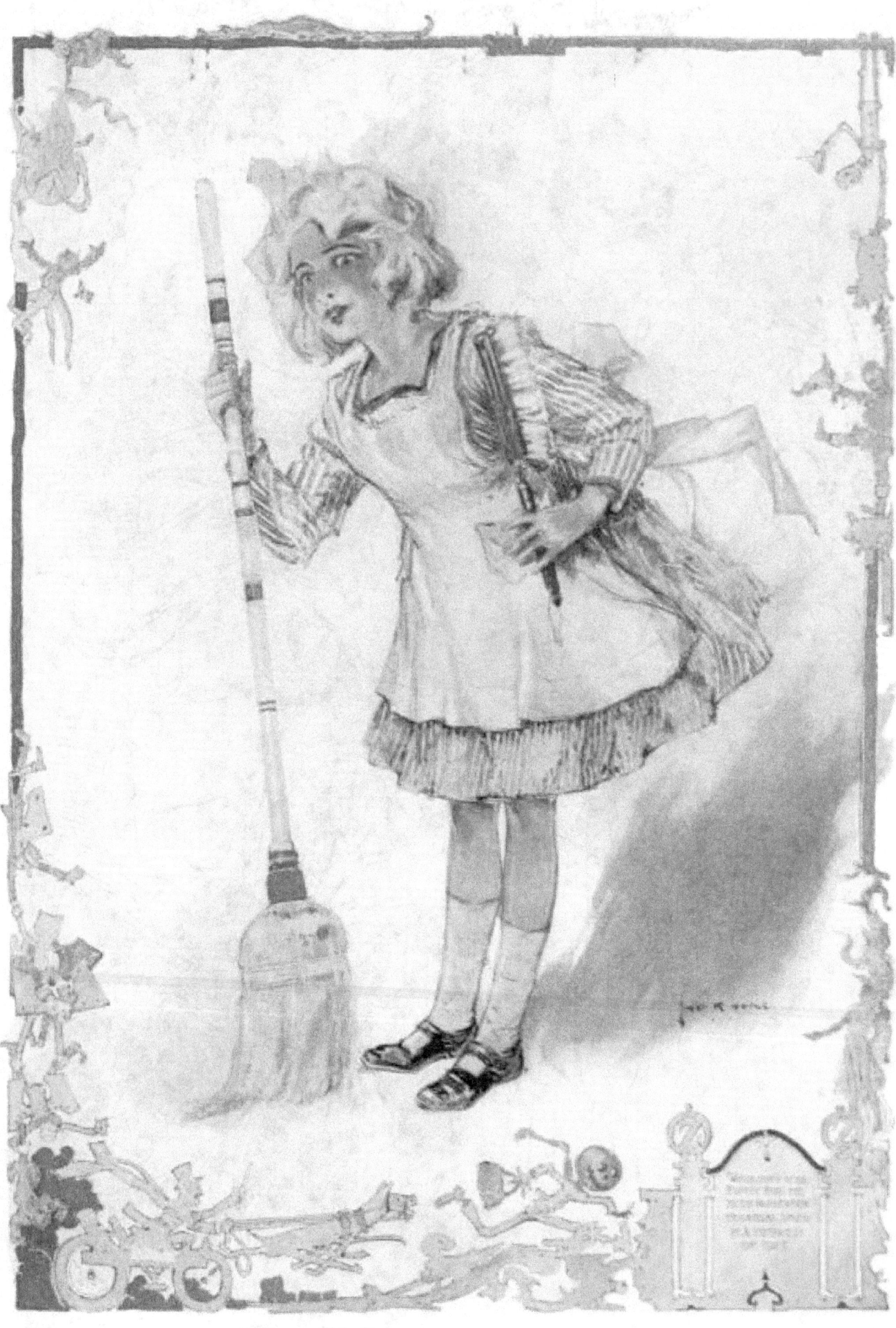

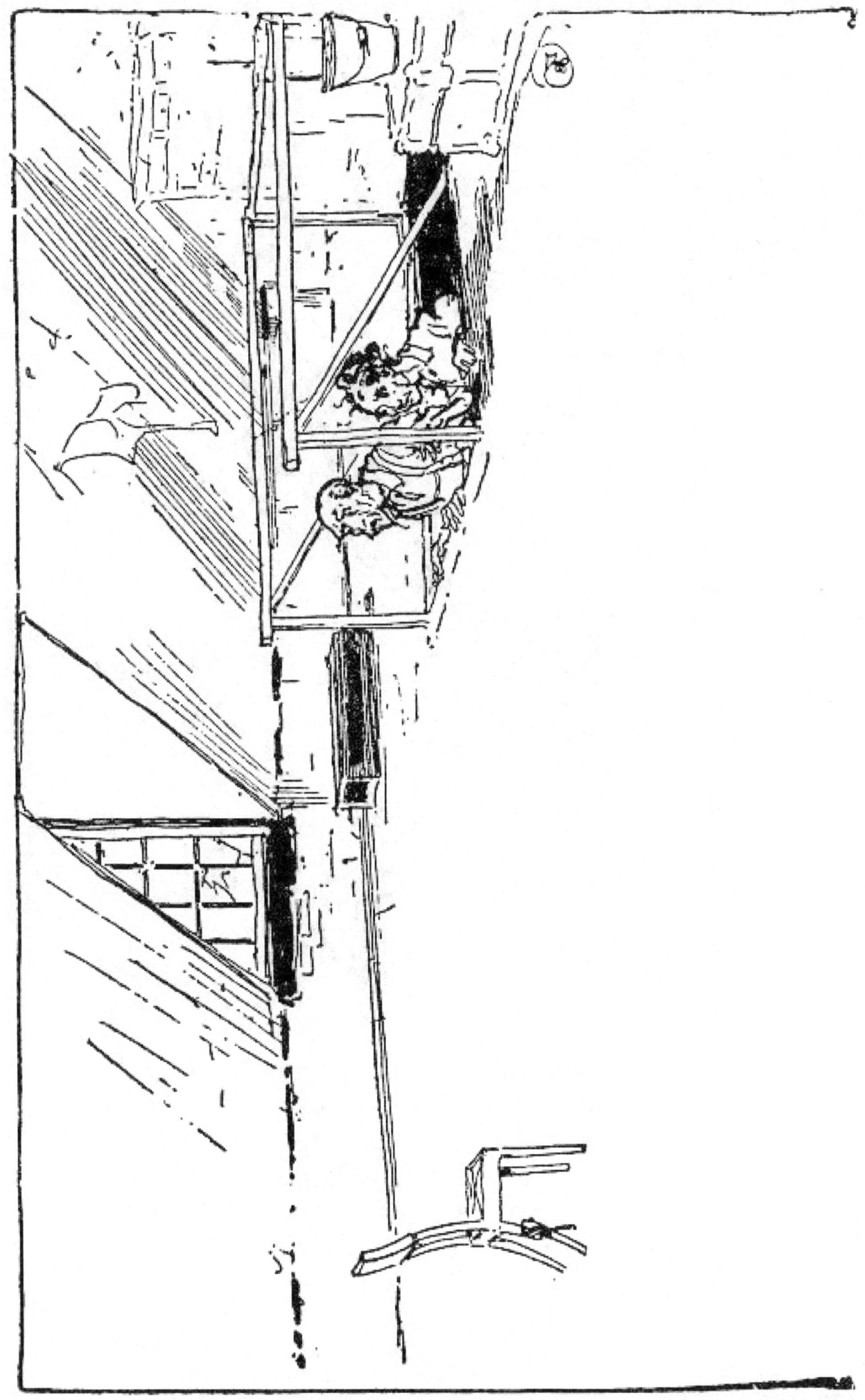

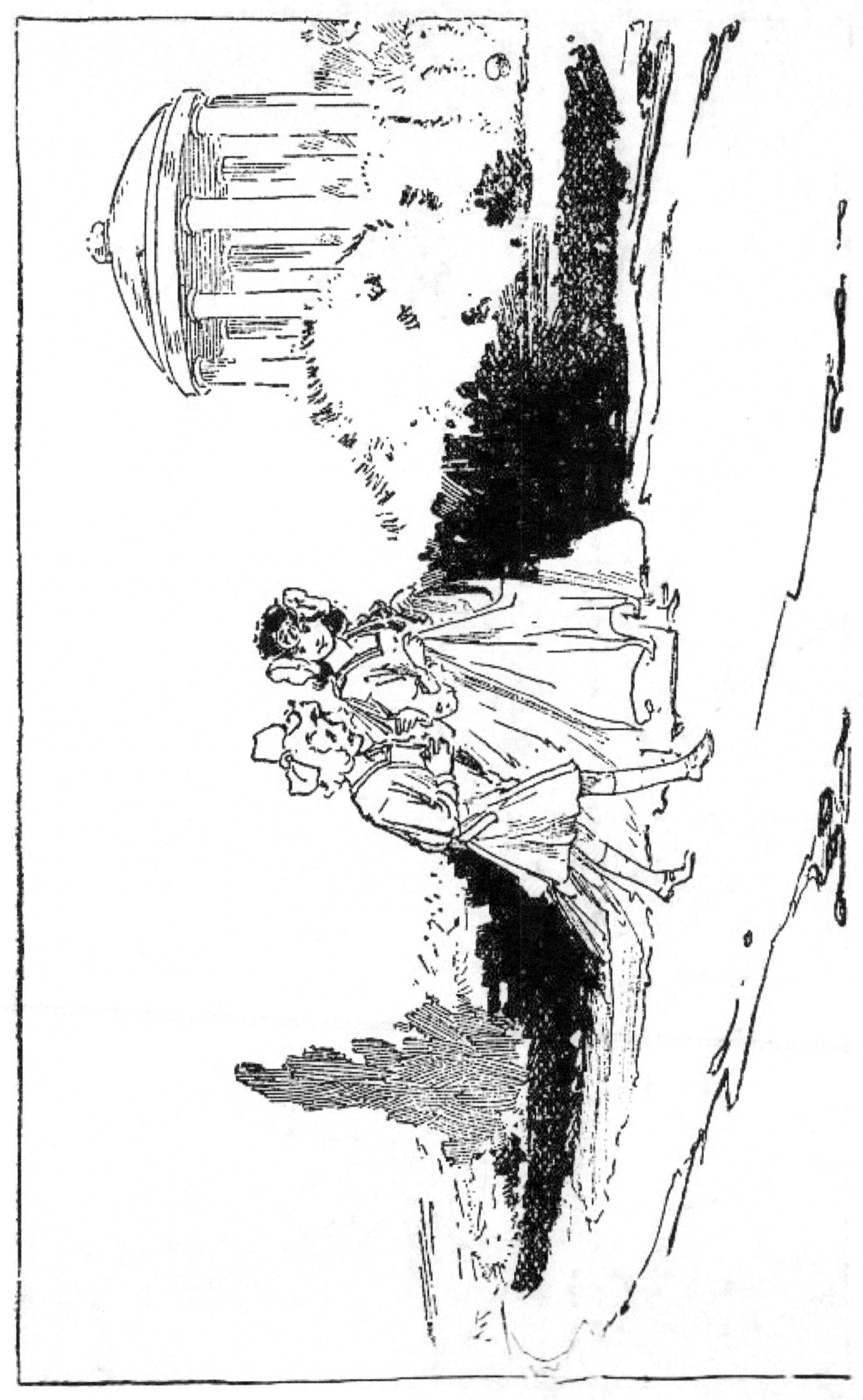

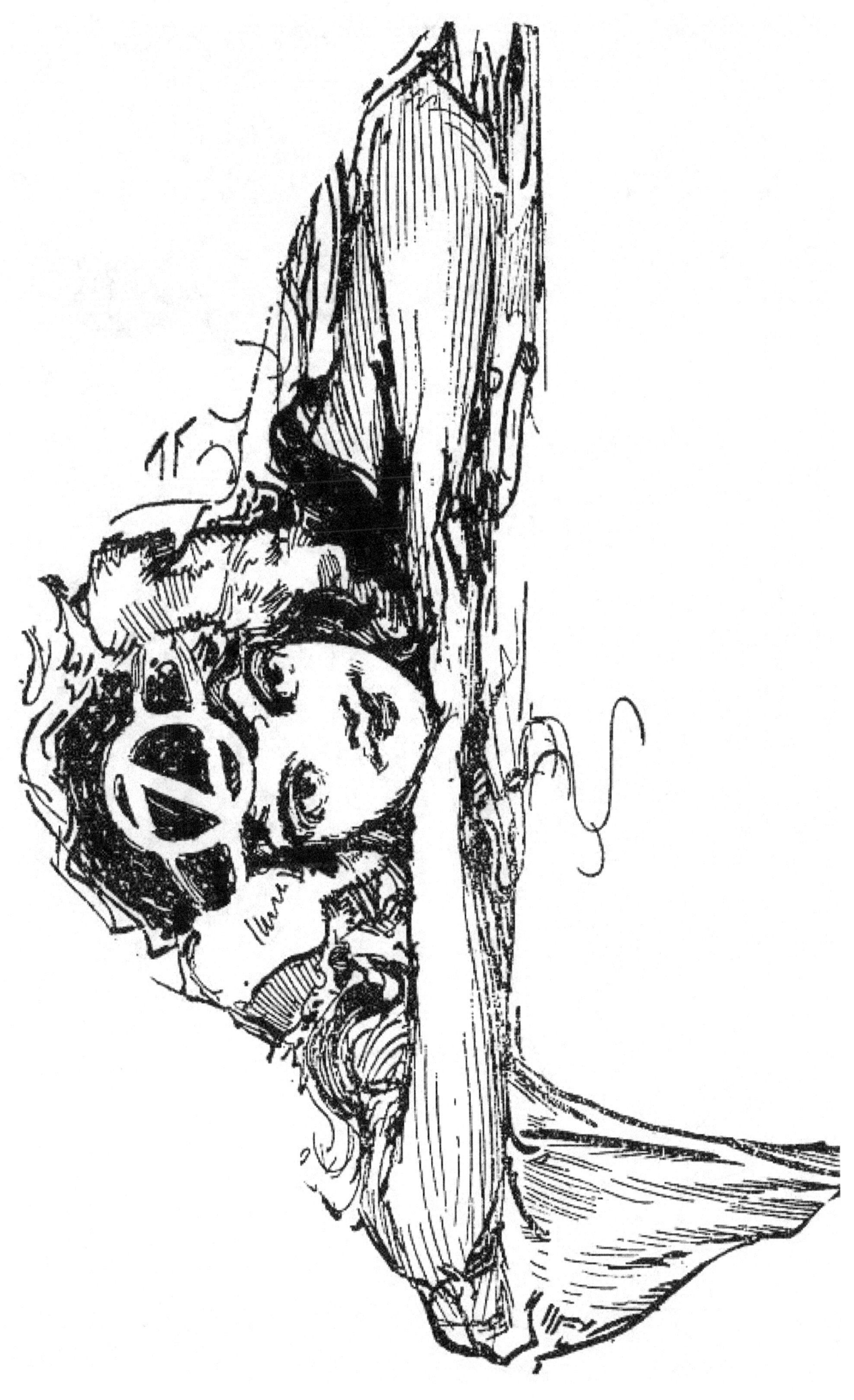

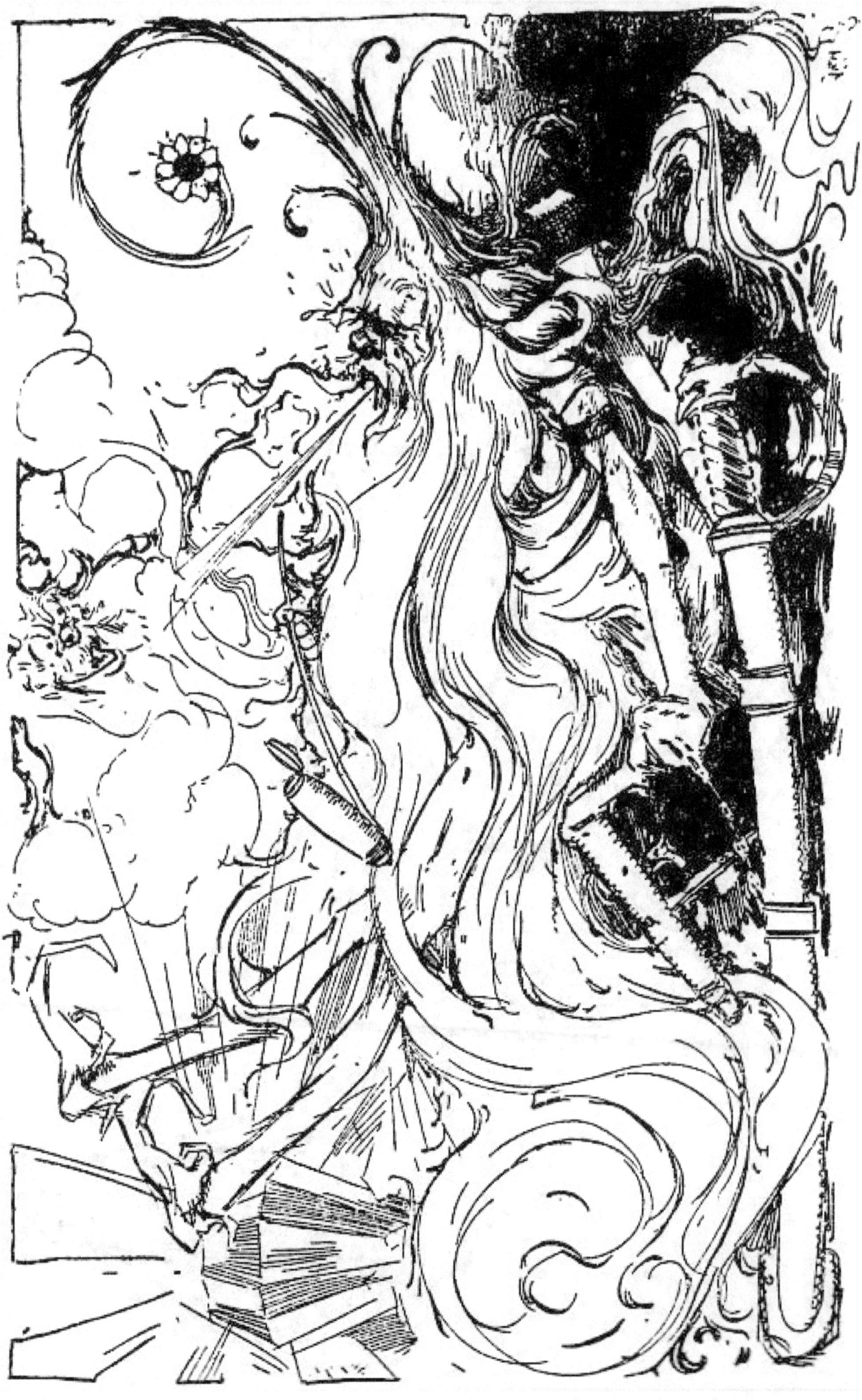

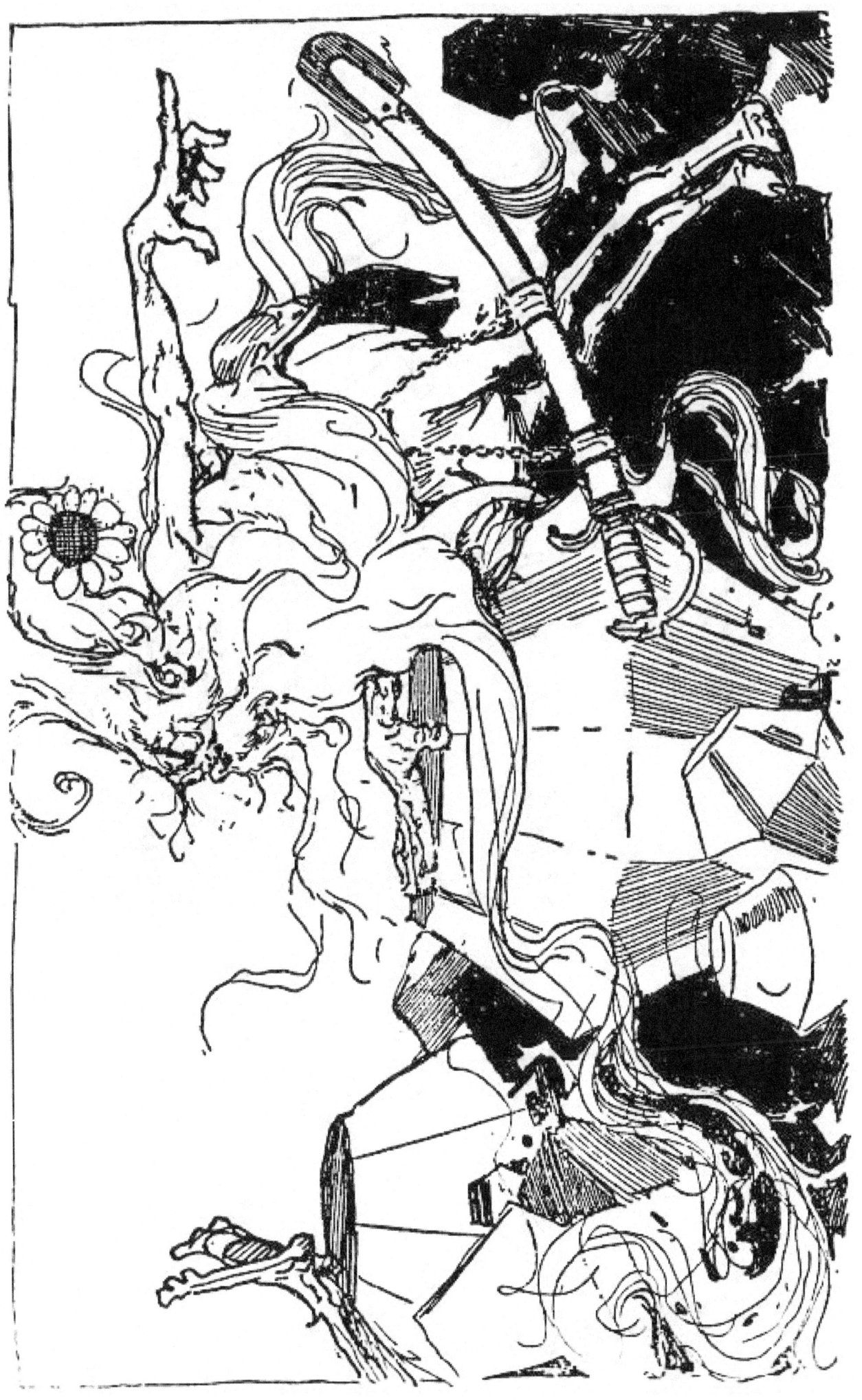

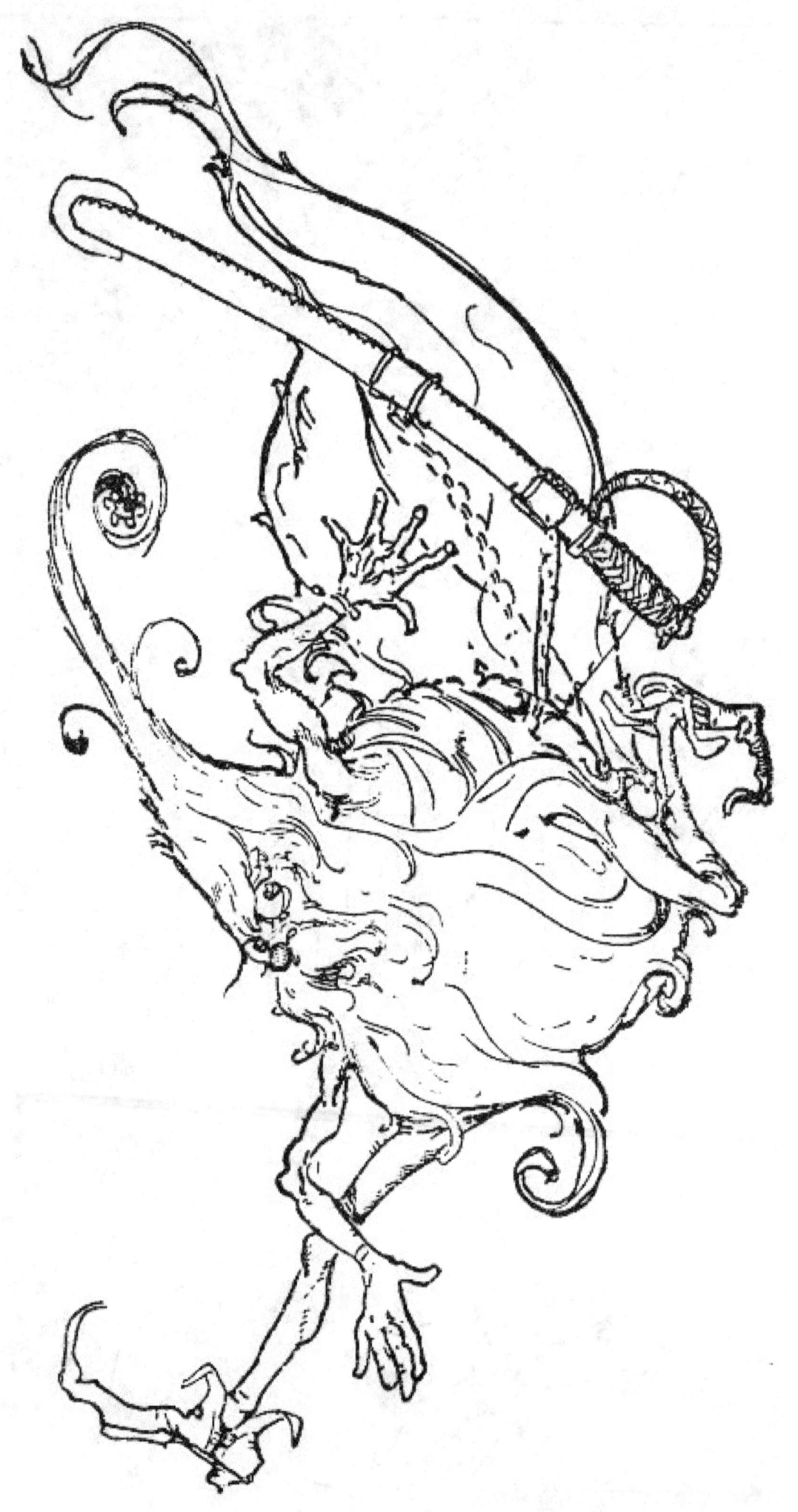

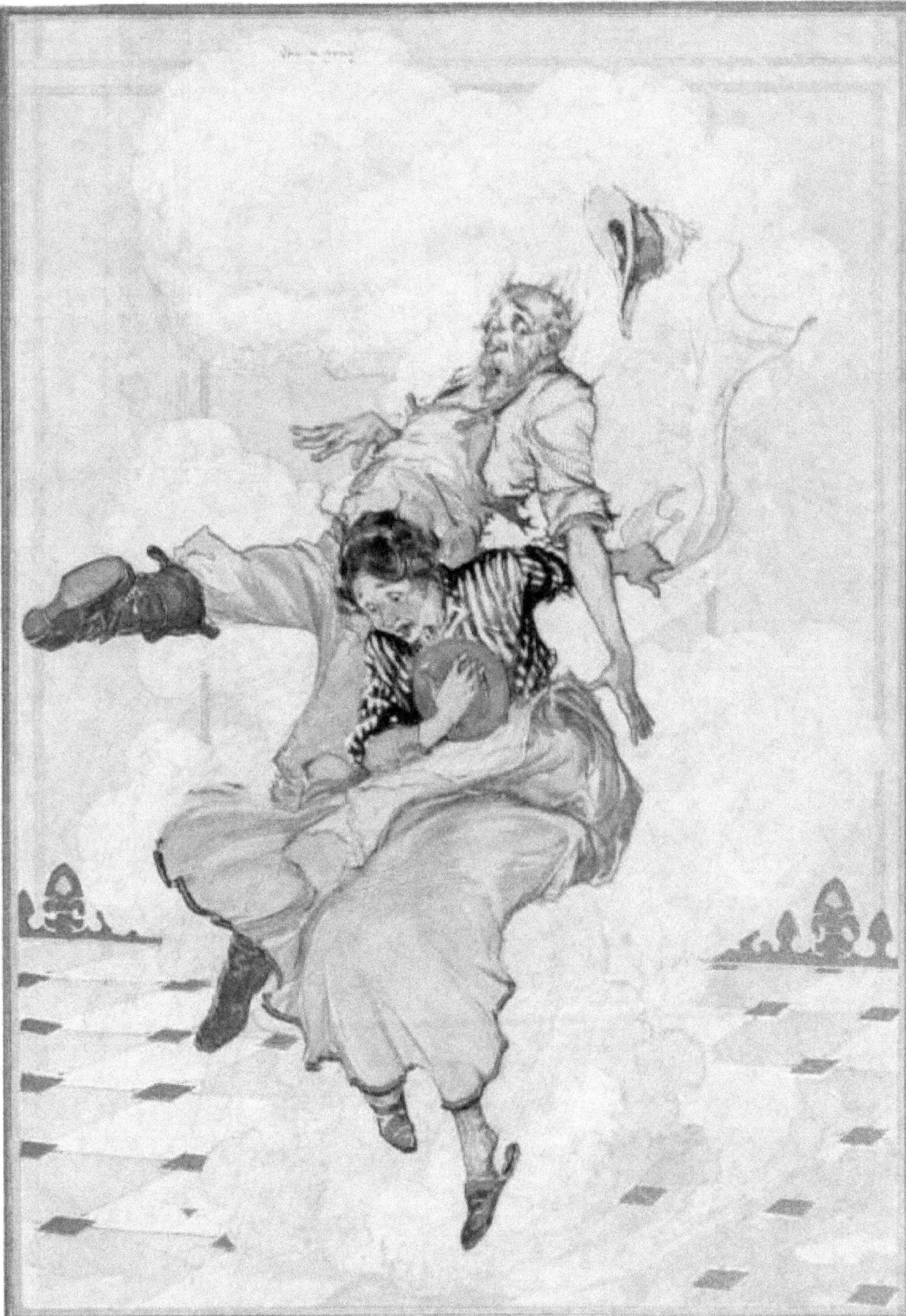

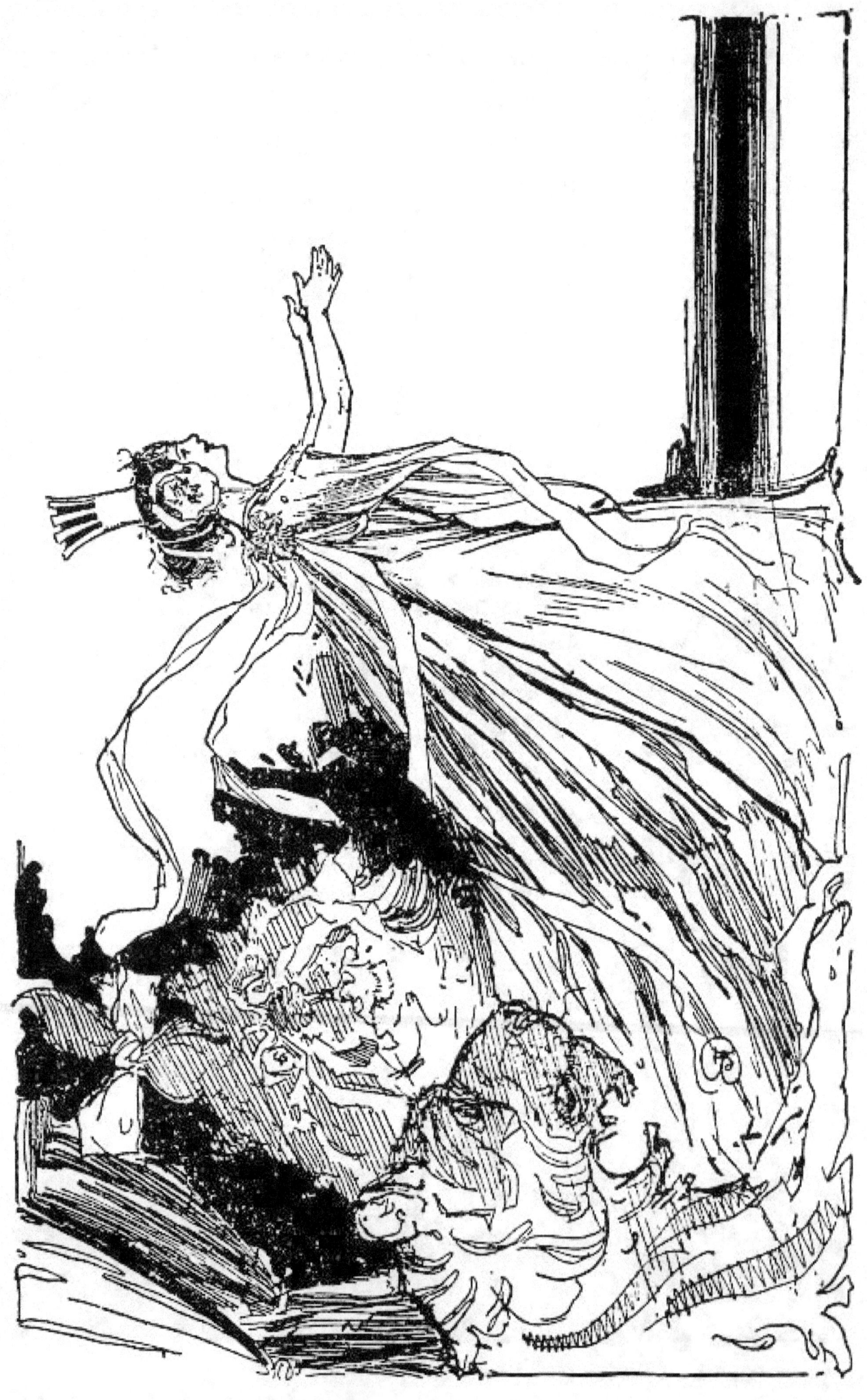

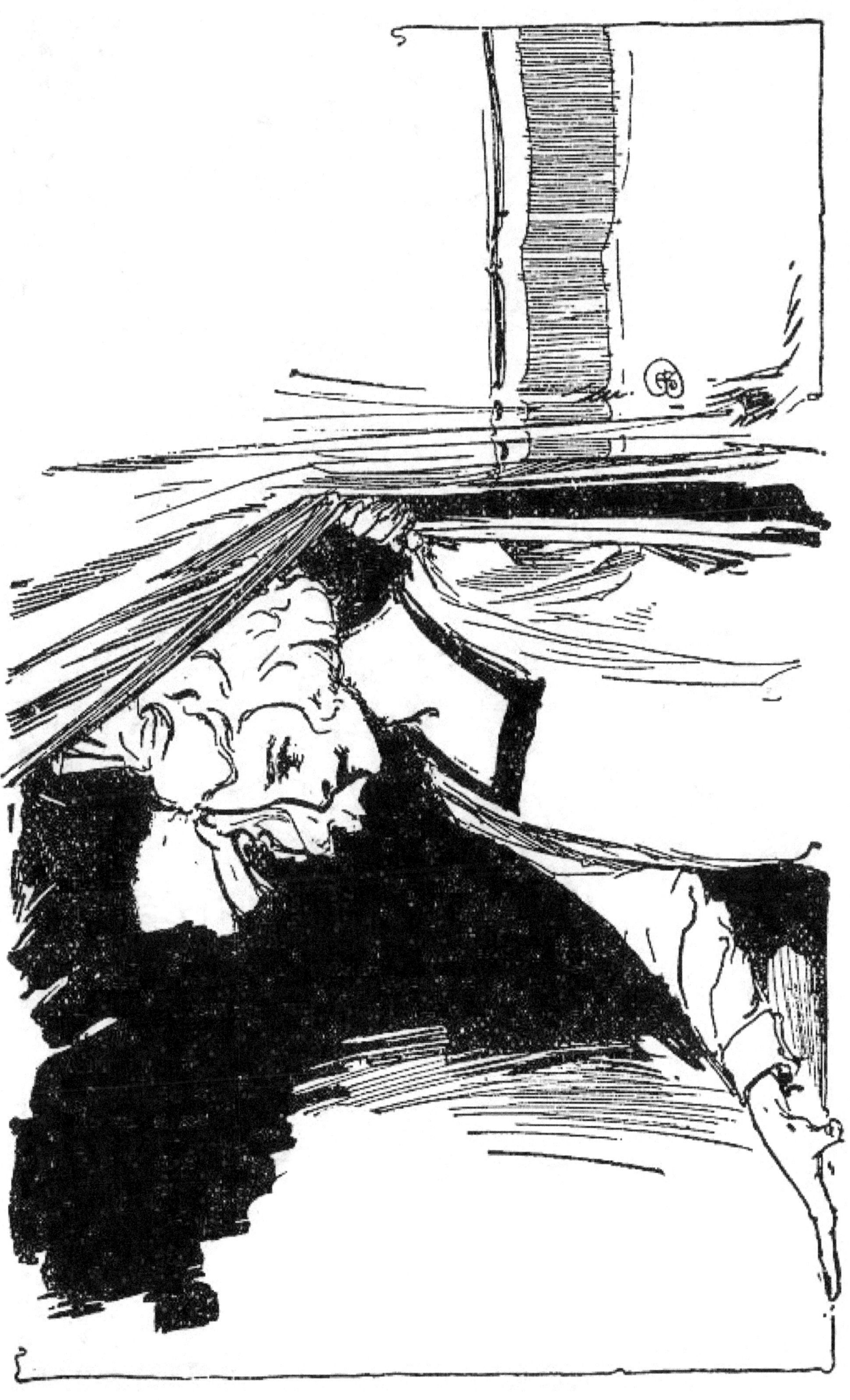

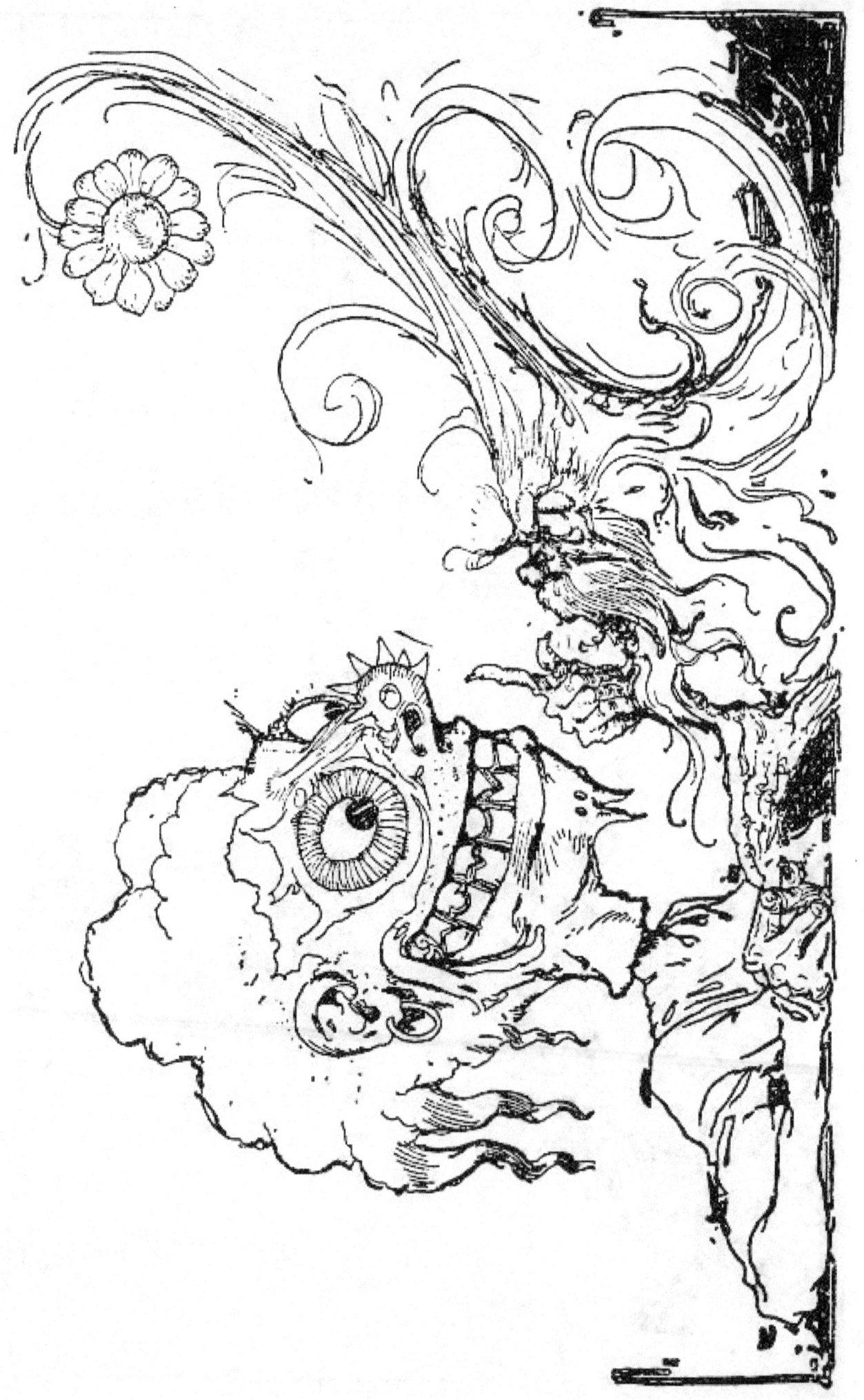

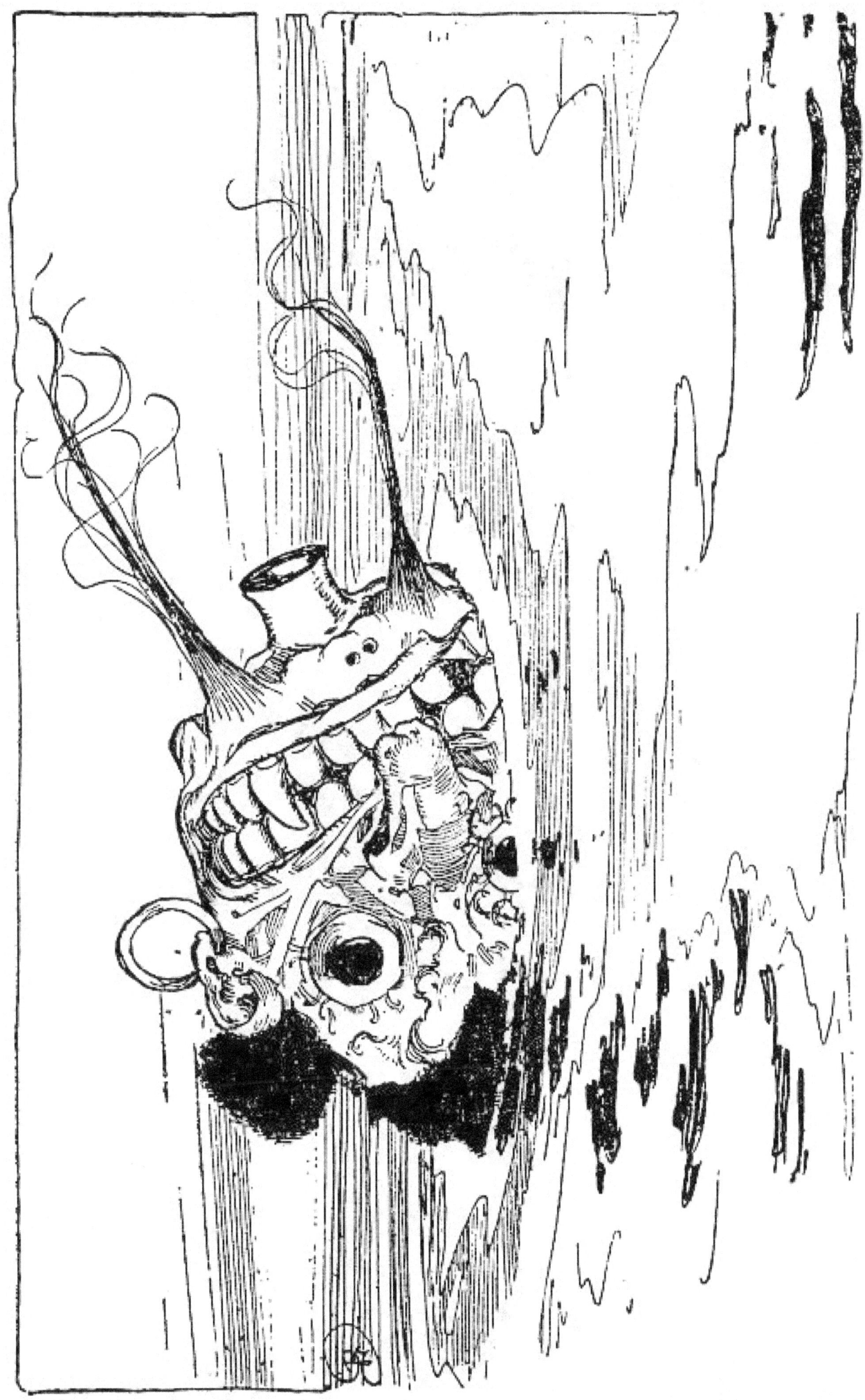

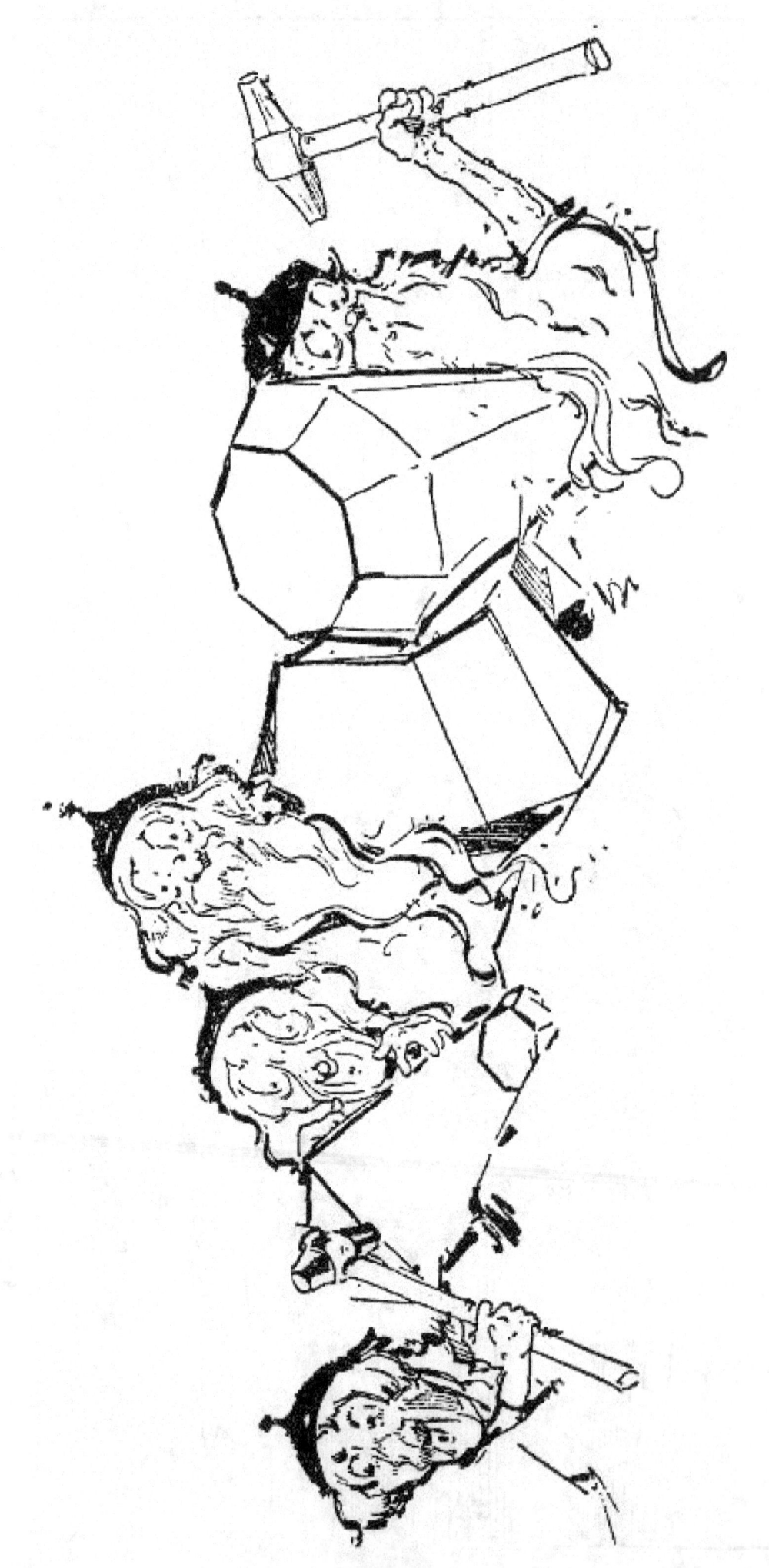

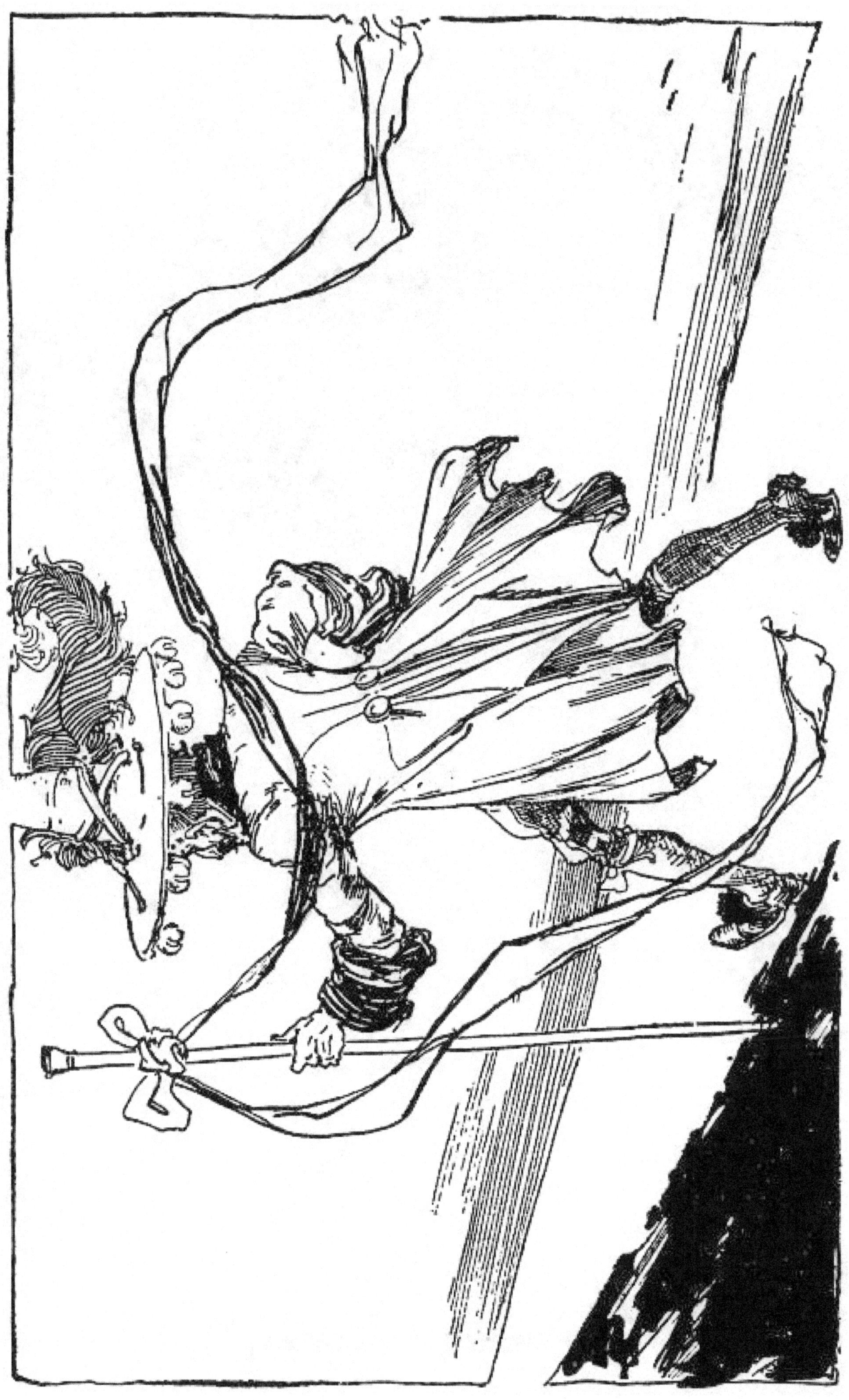

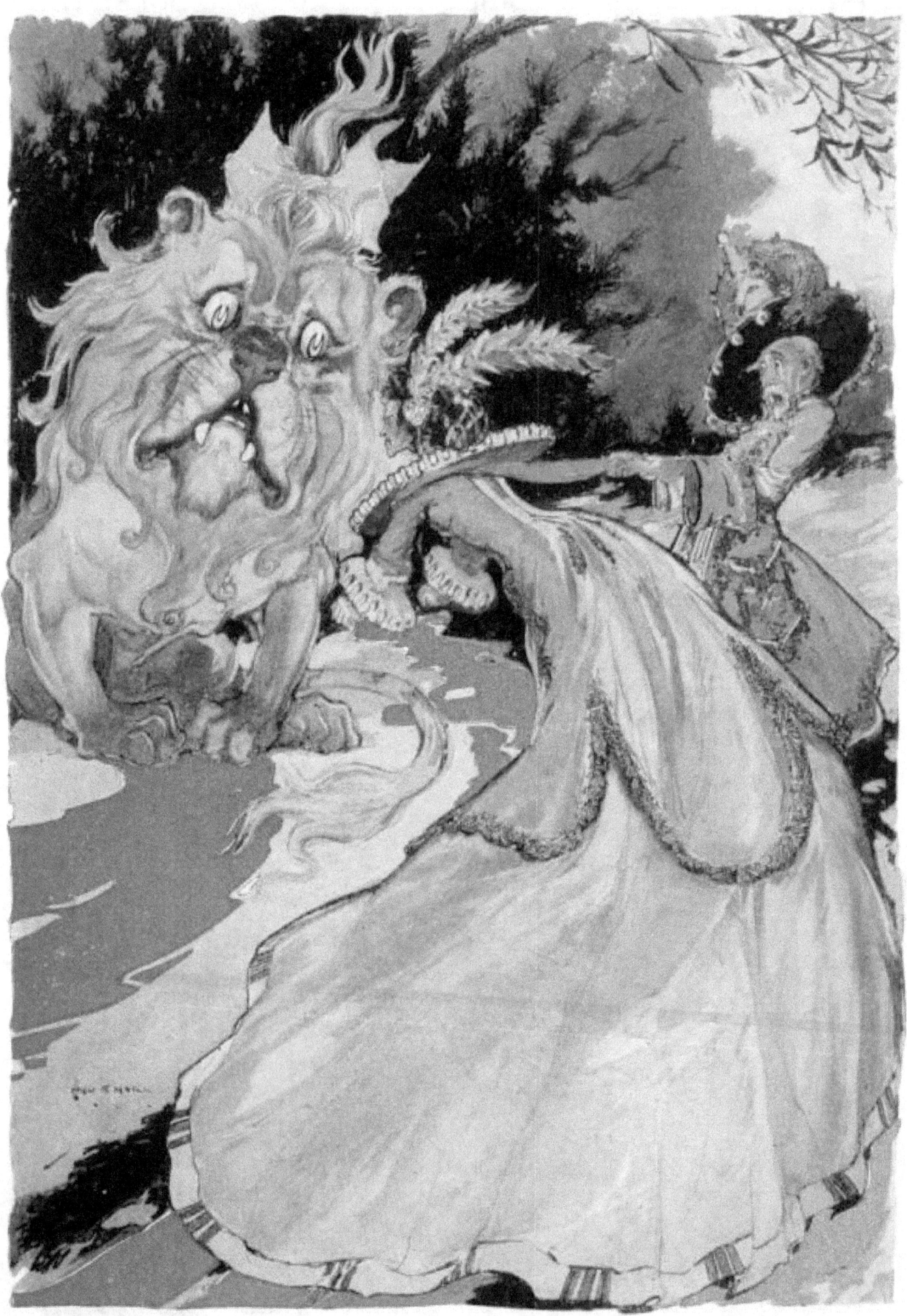

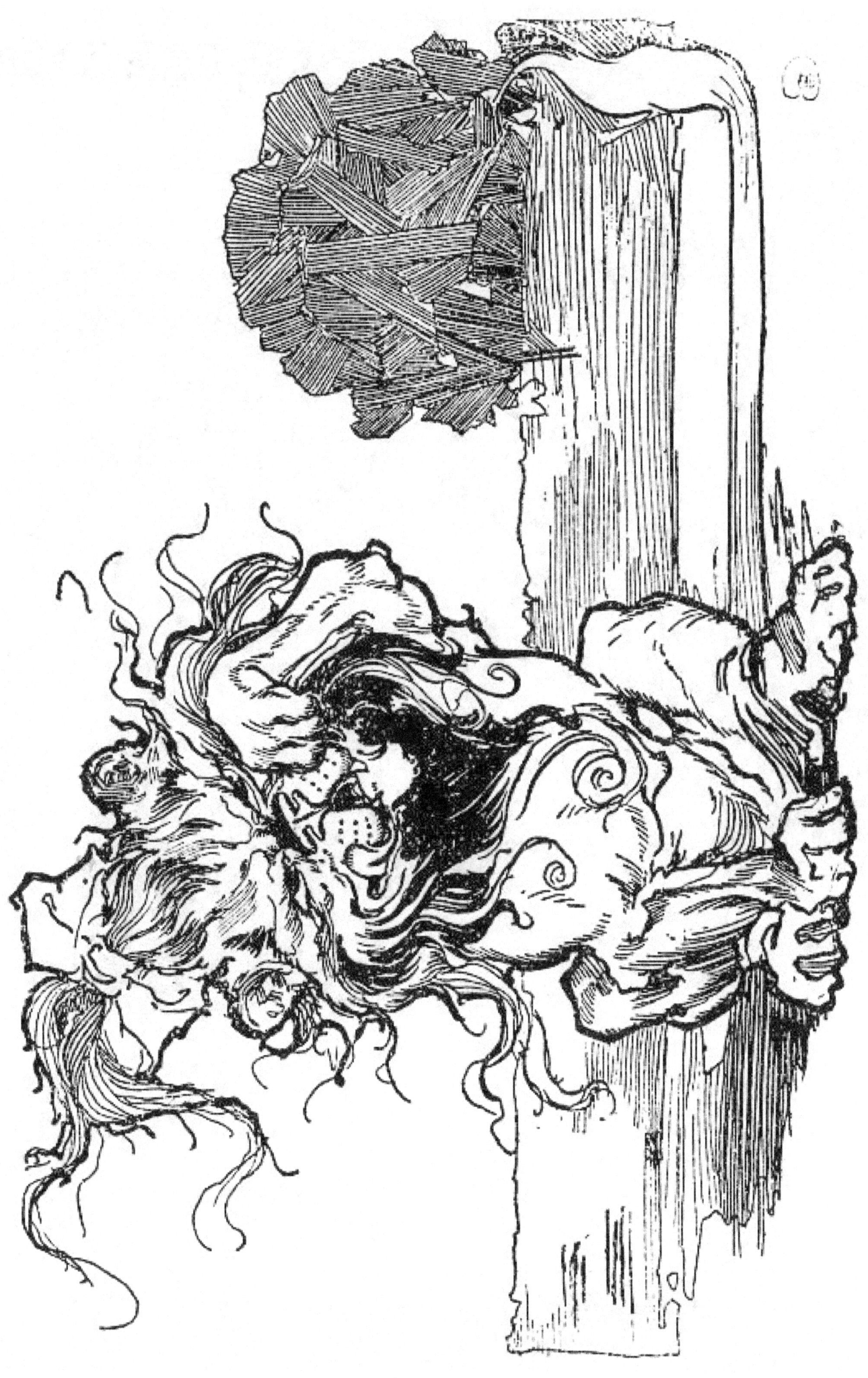

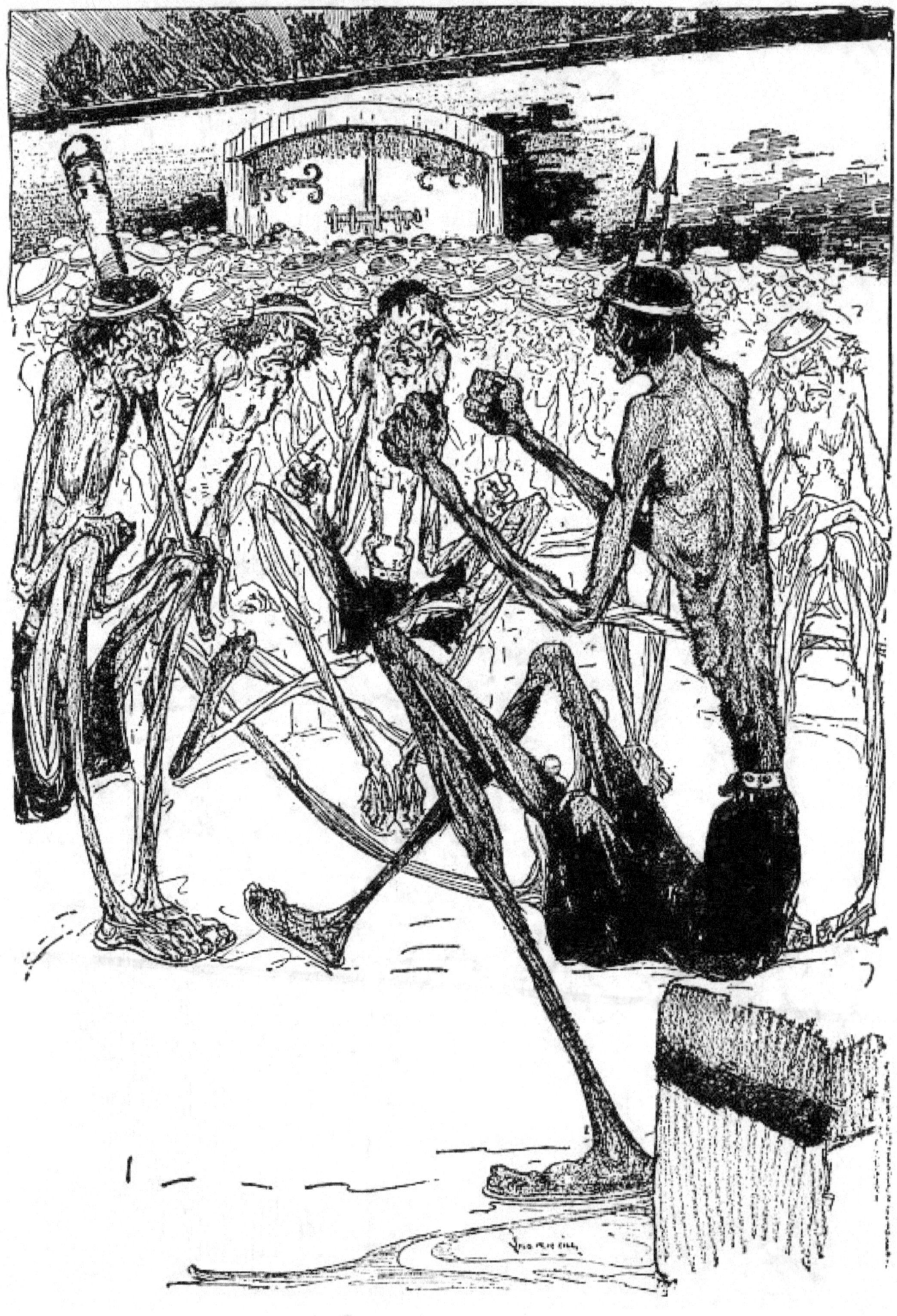

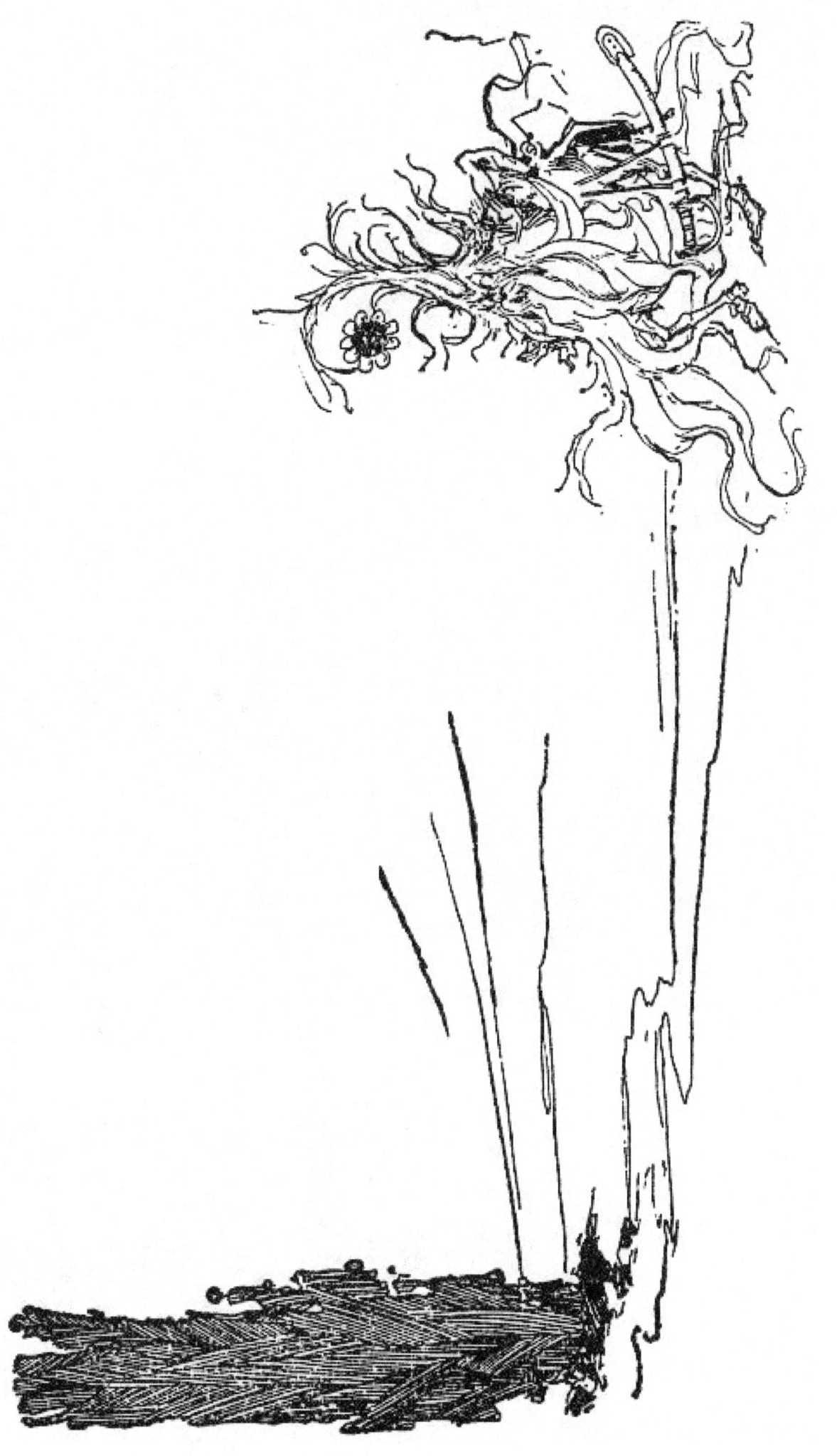

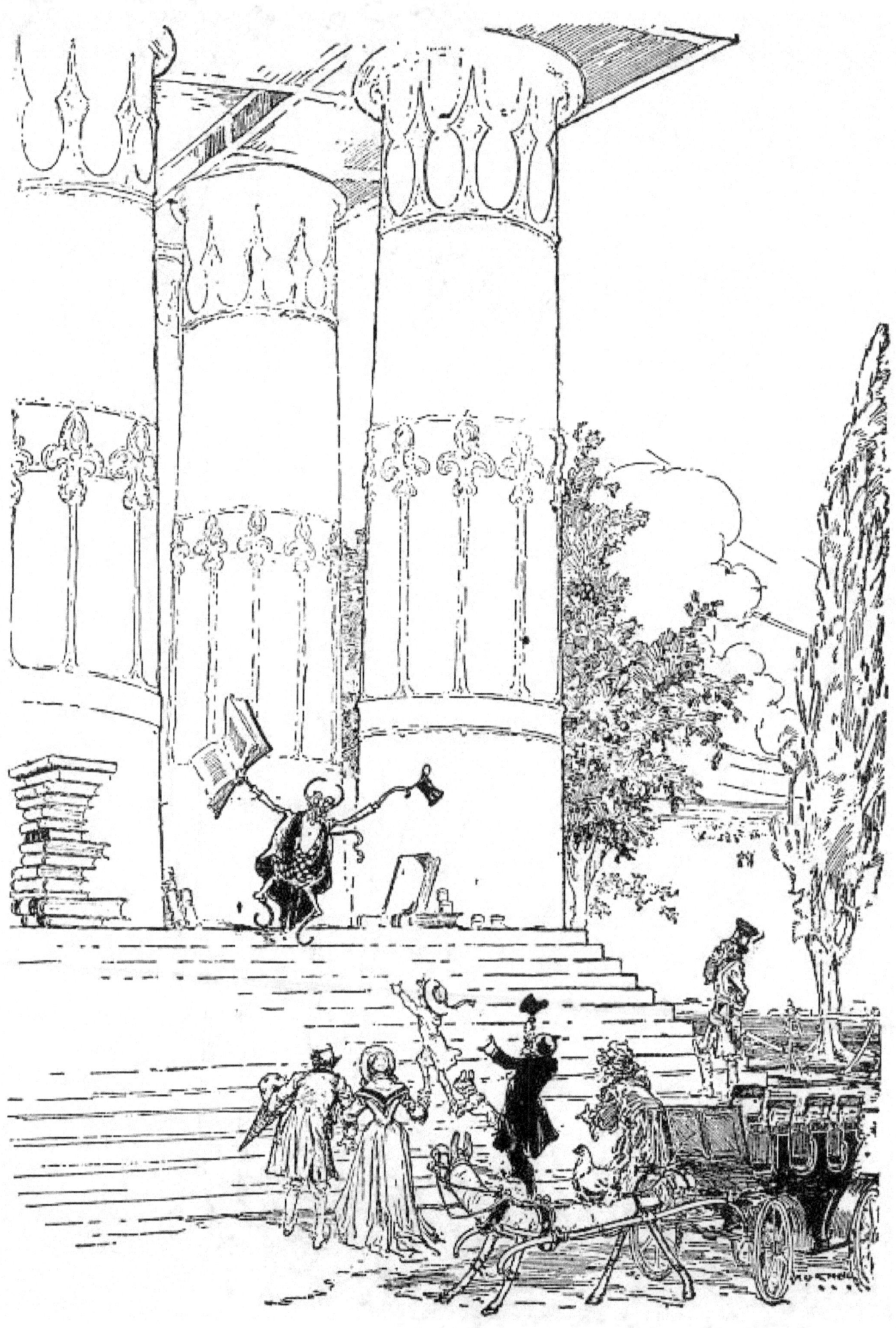

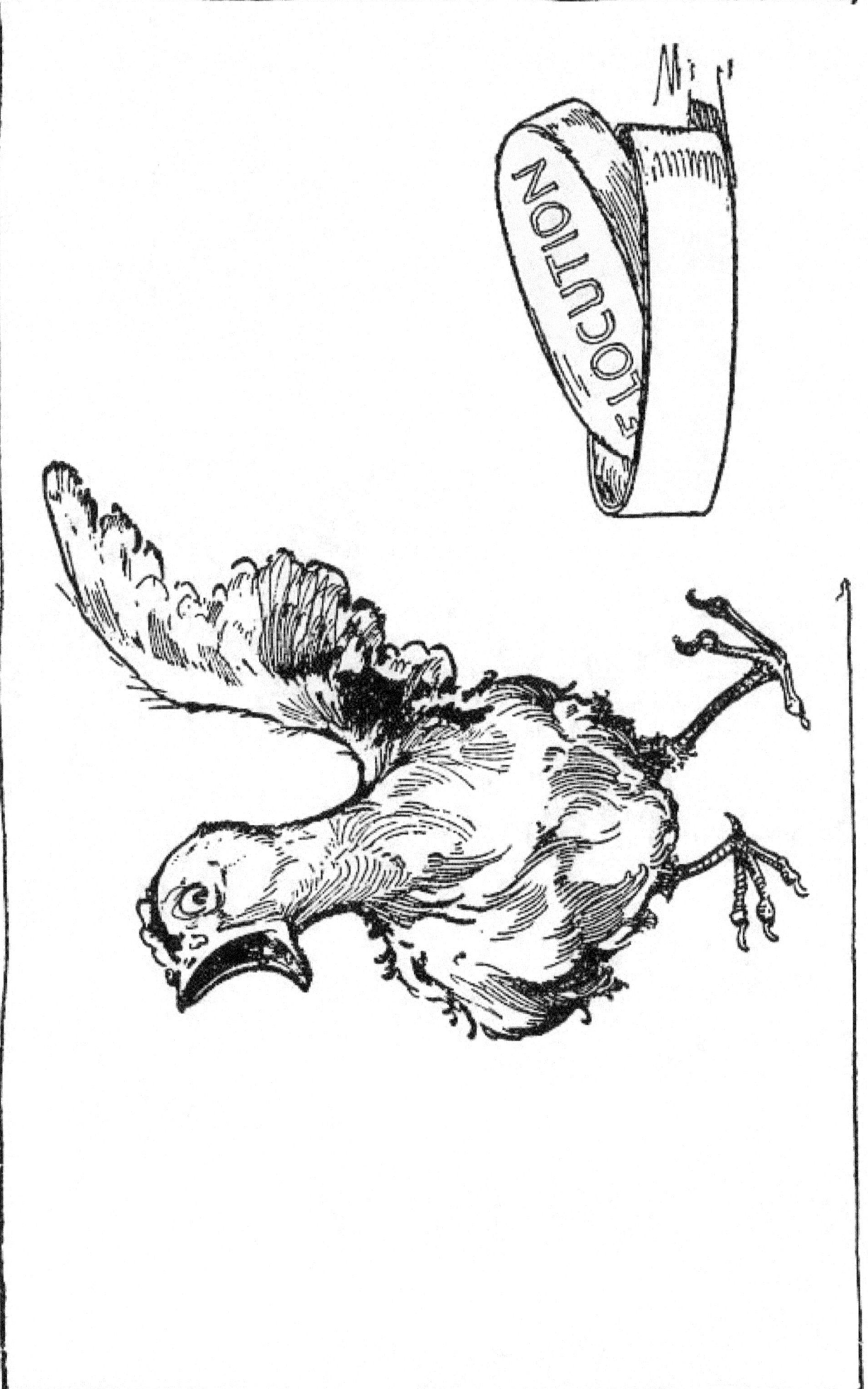

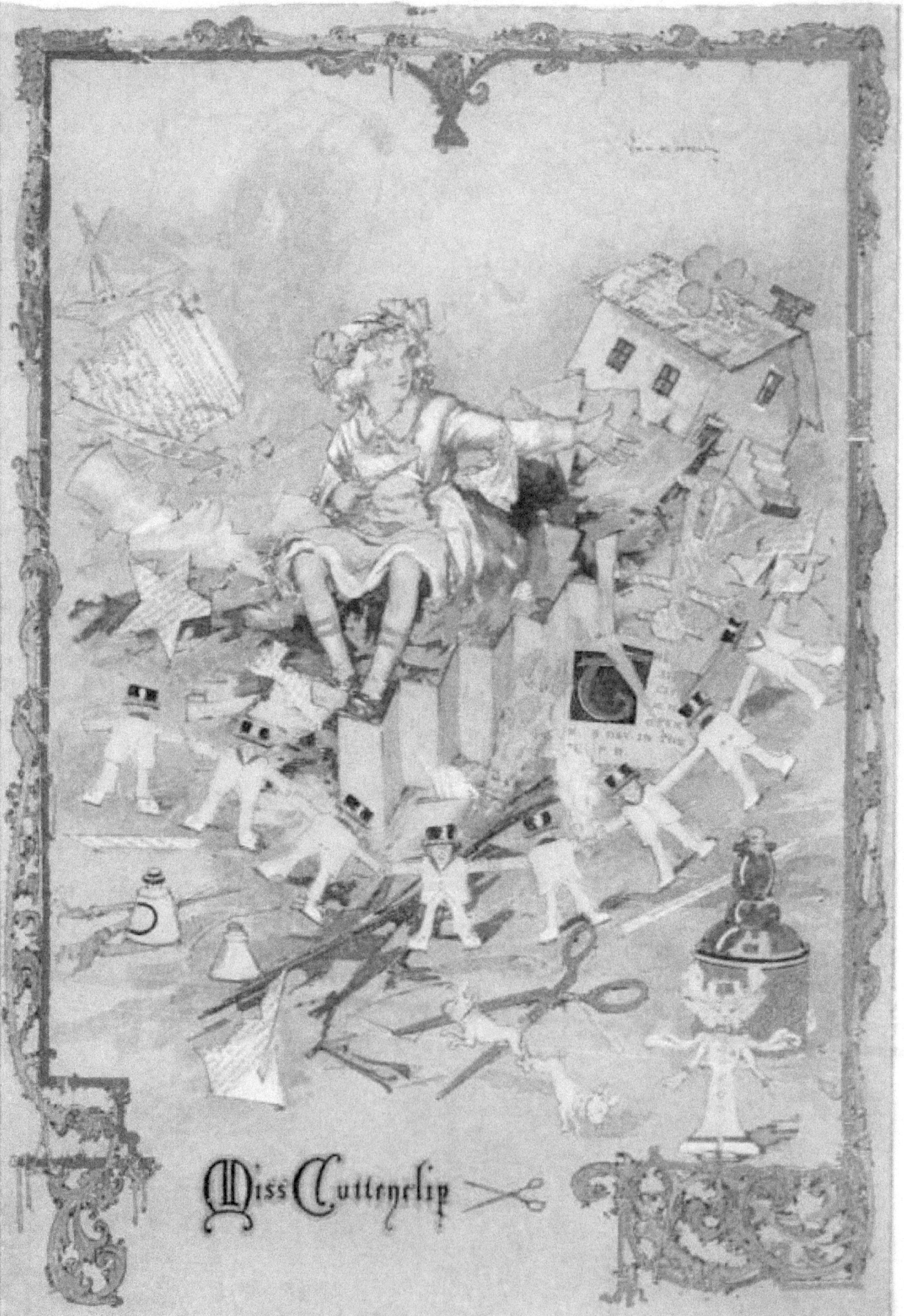

Miss Cuttenclip

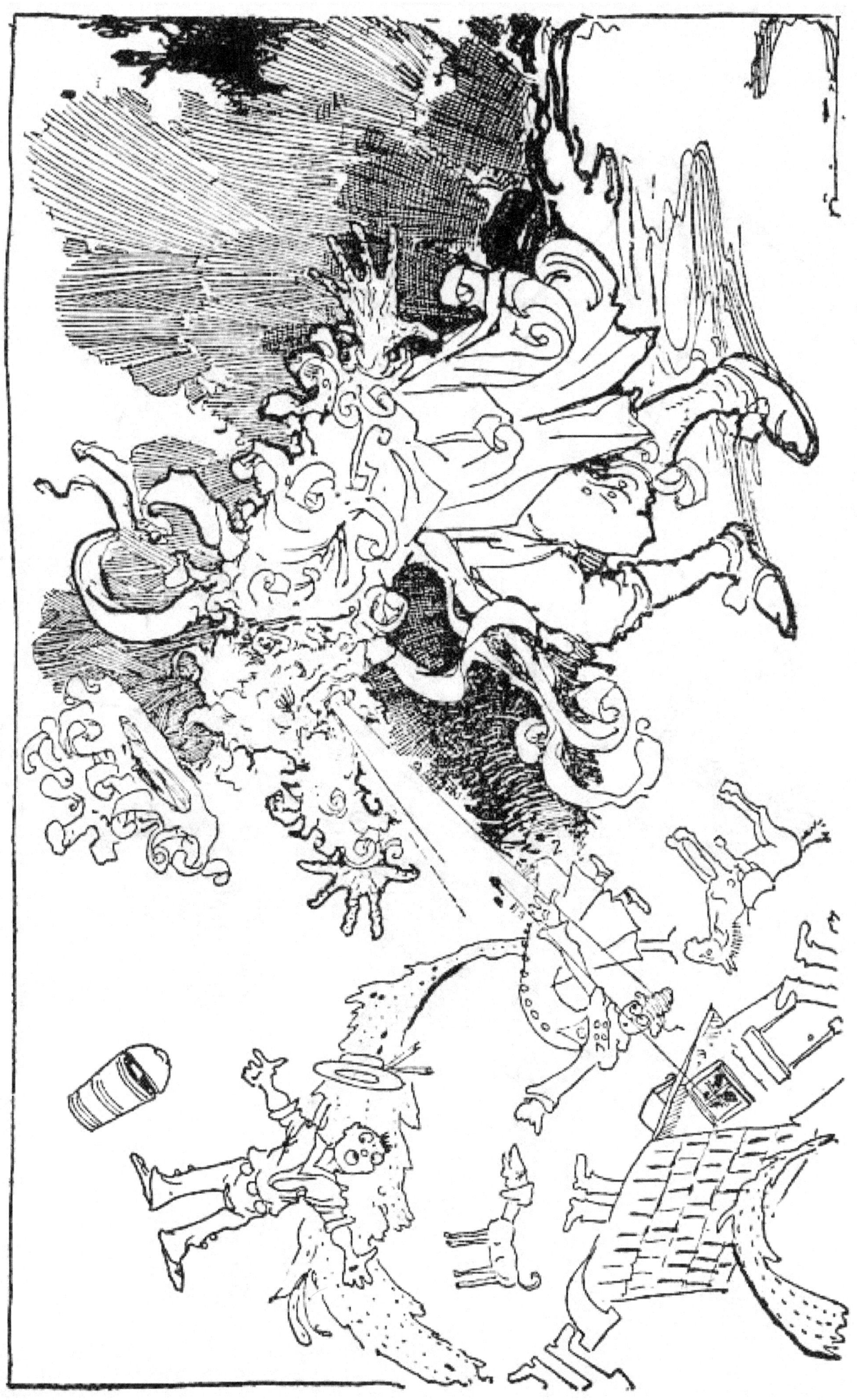

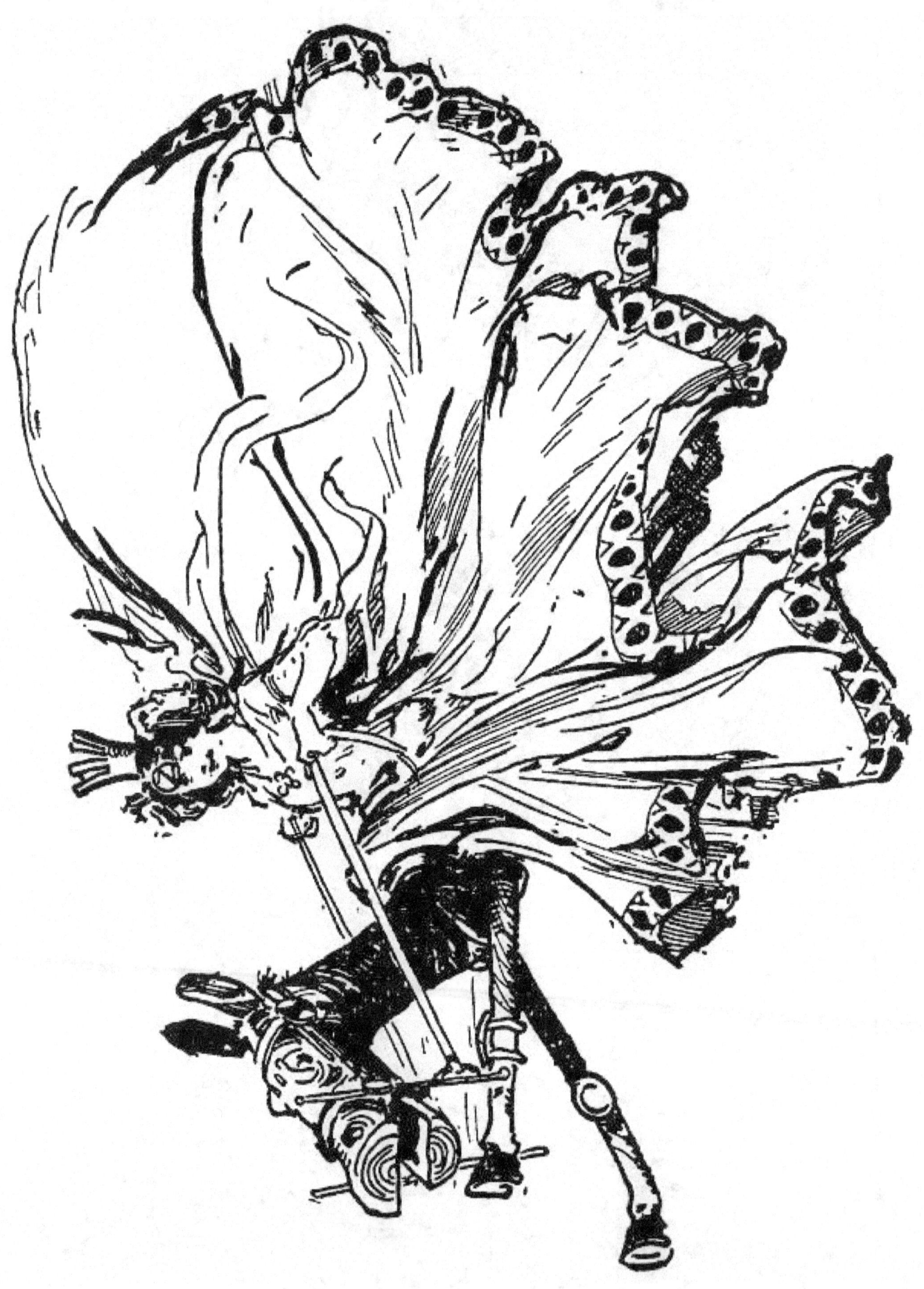

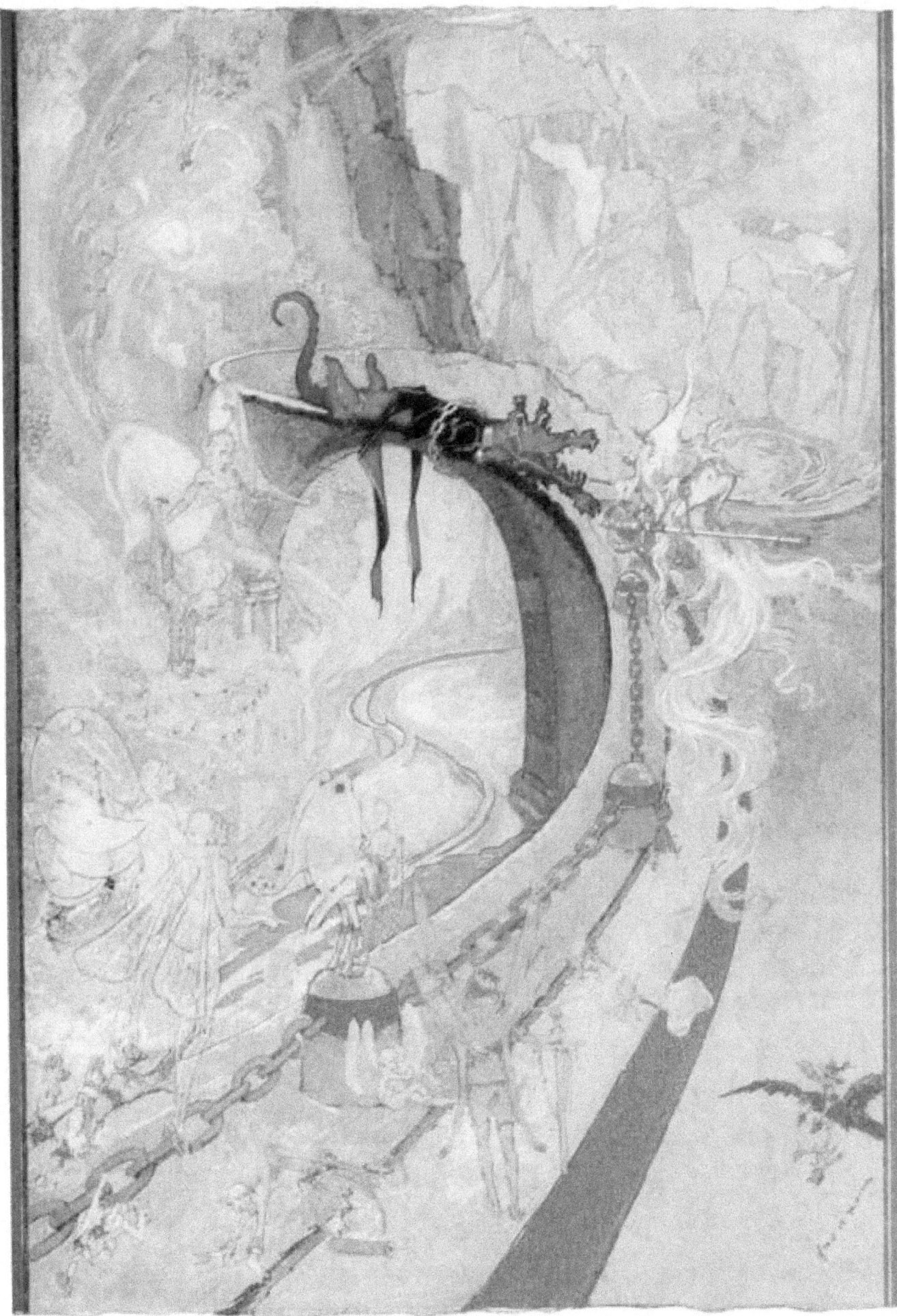

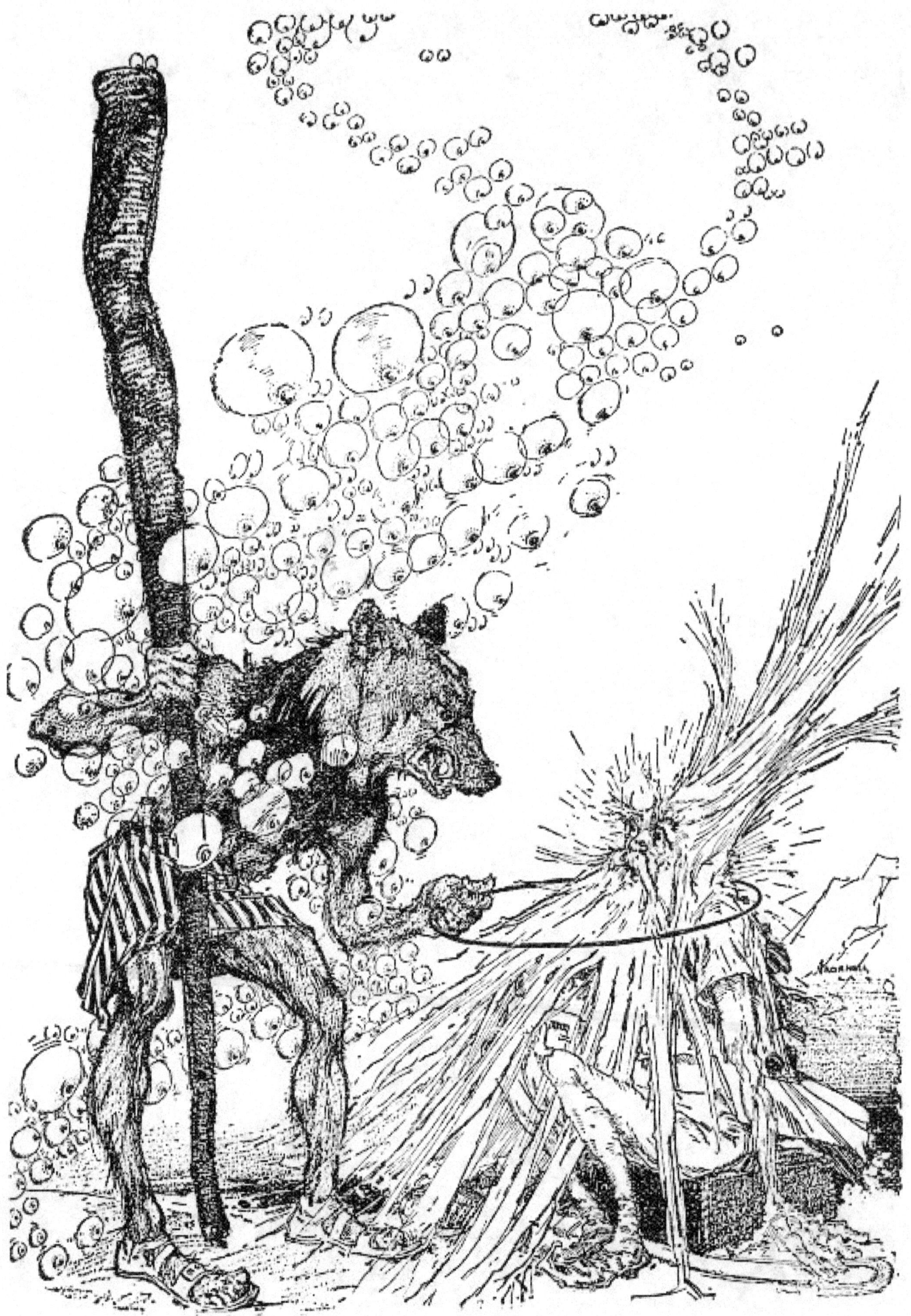

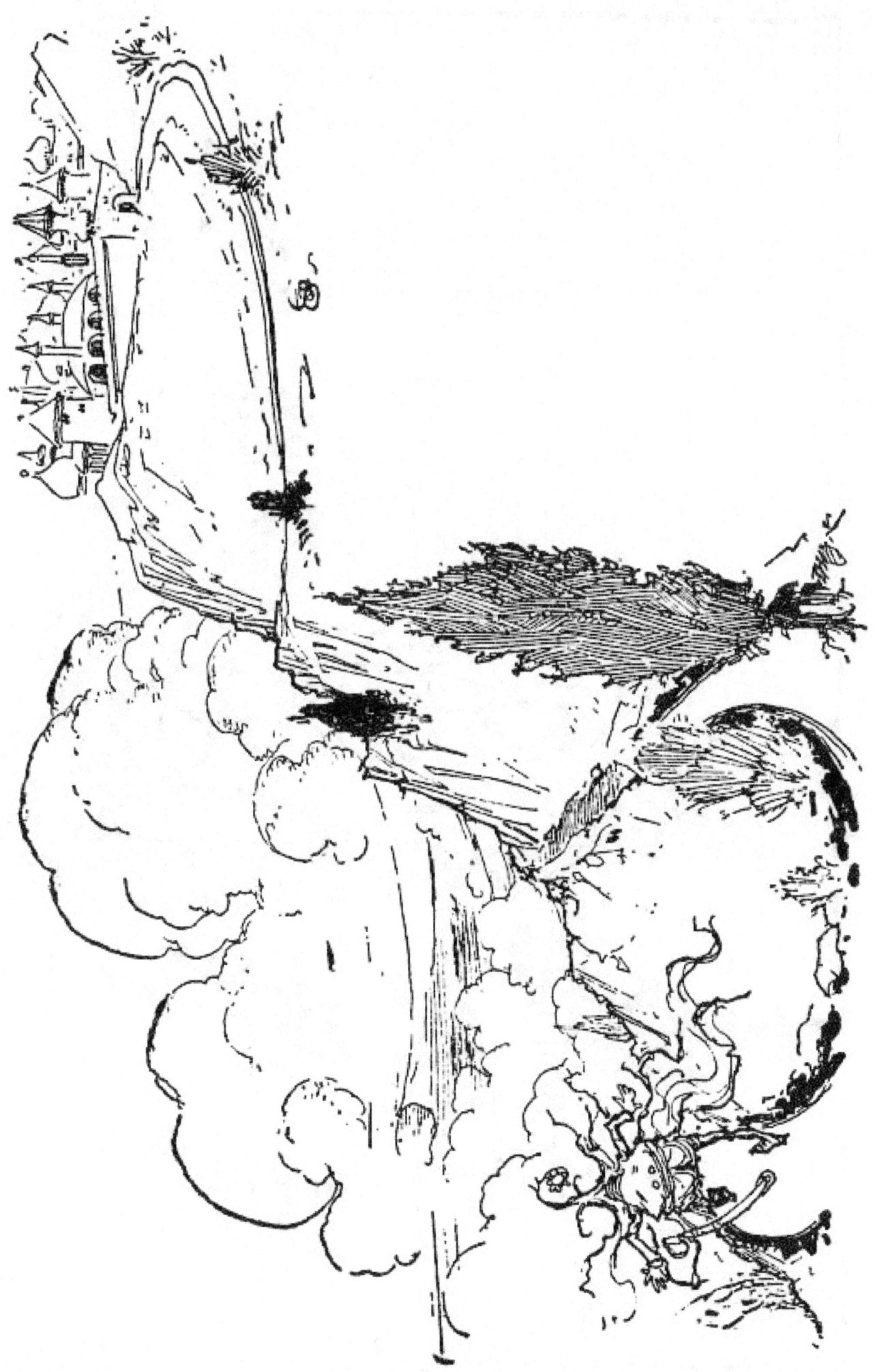

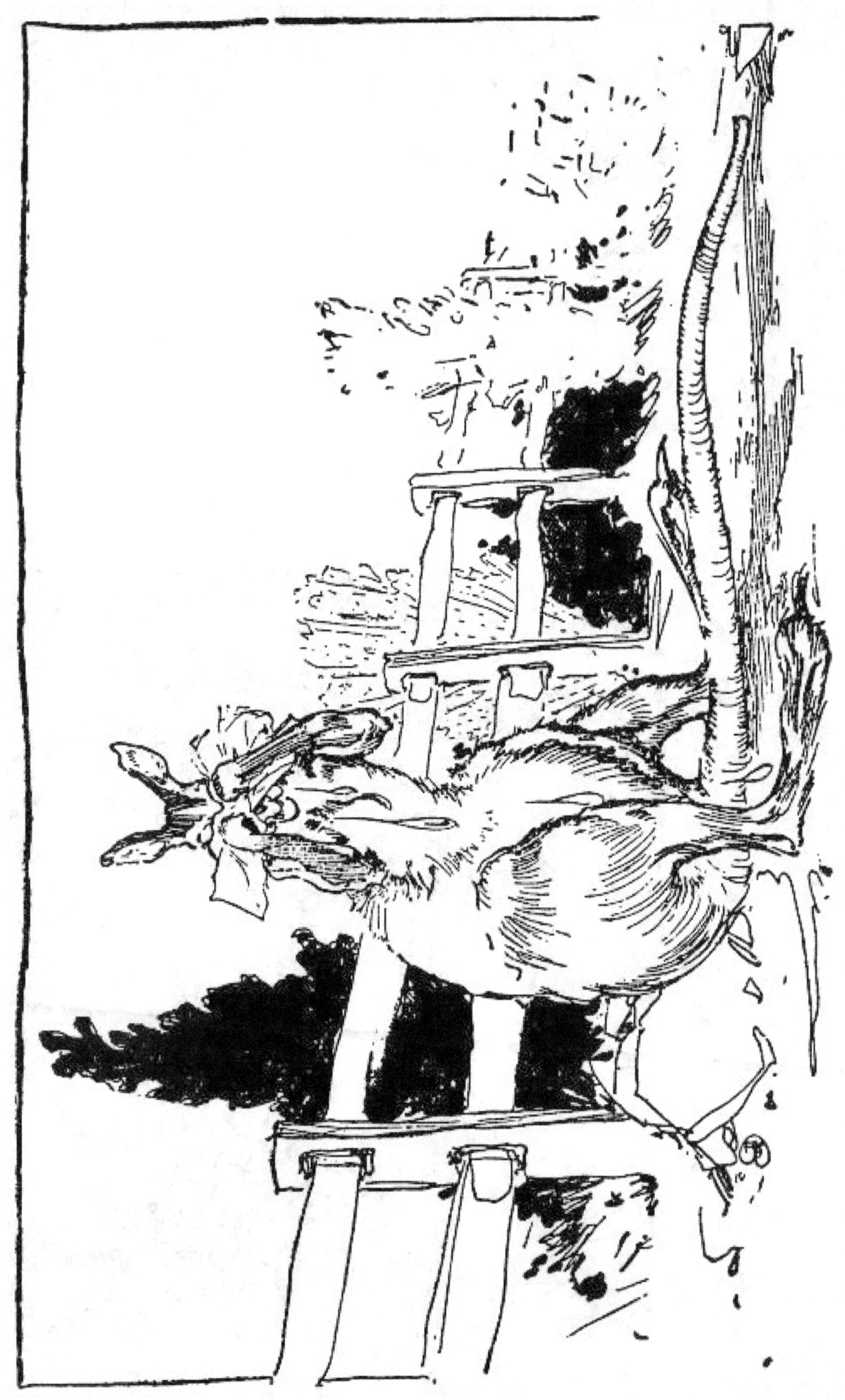

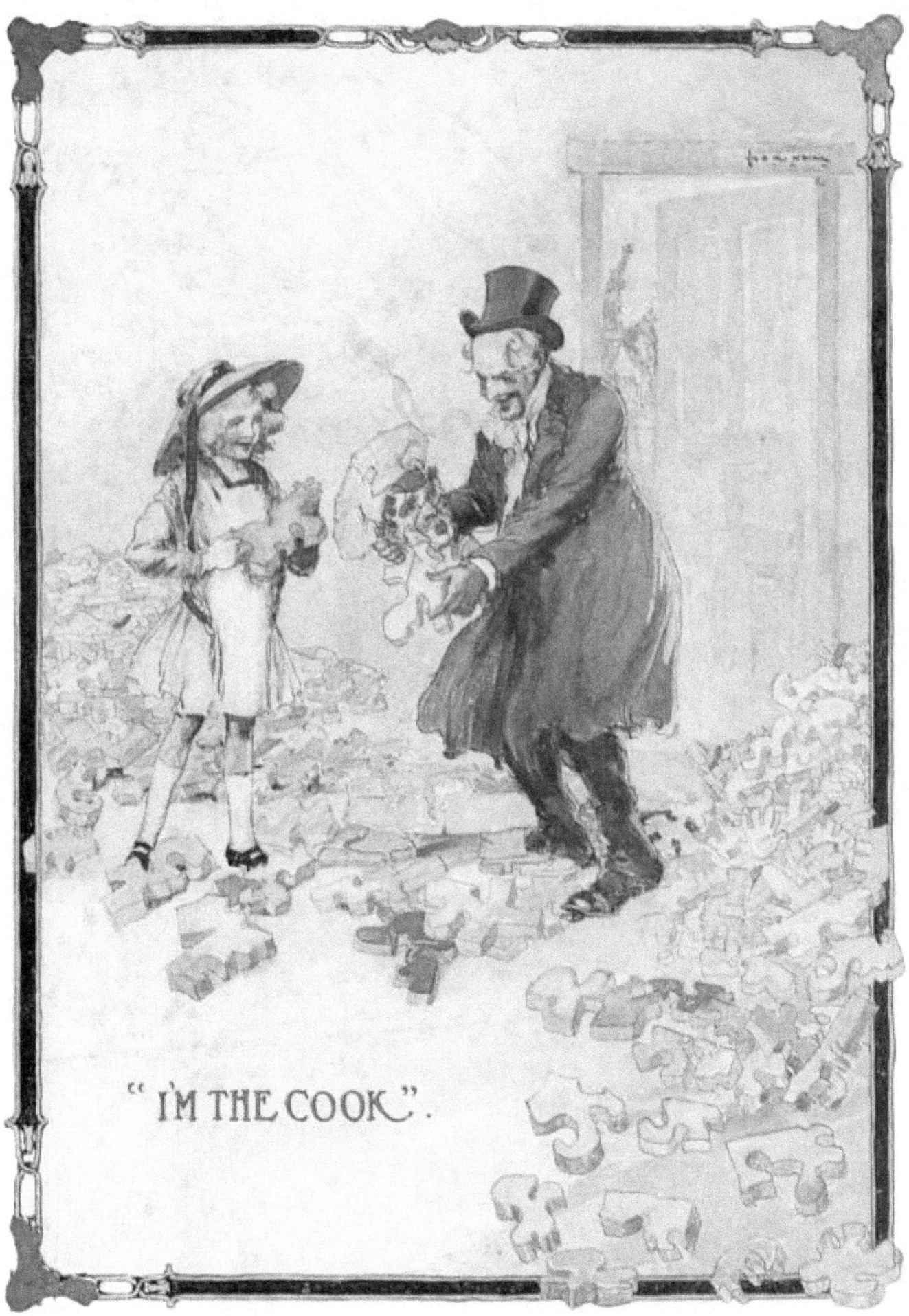

"I'M THE COOK".

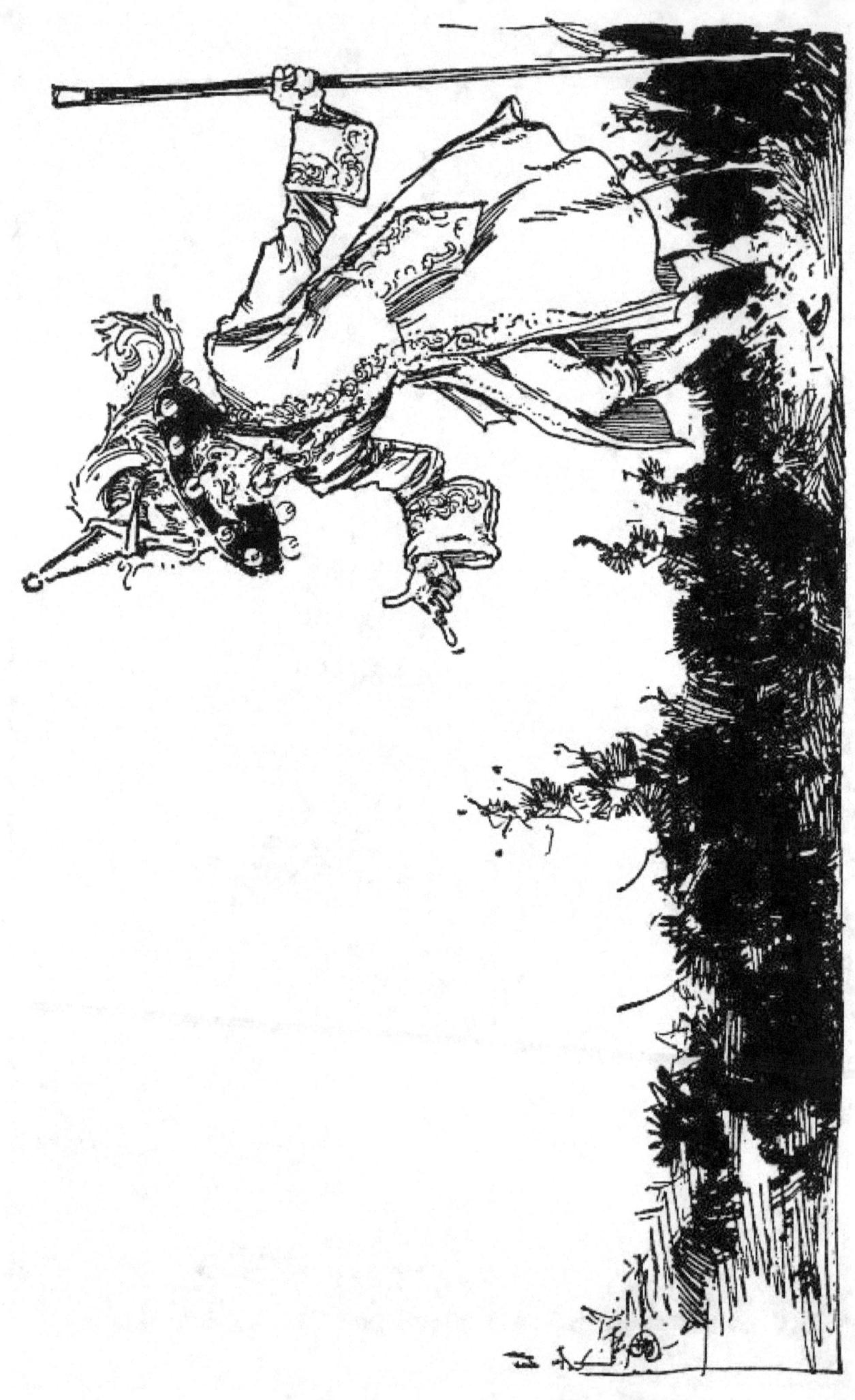

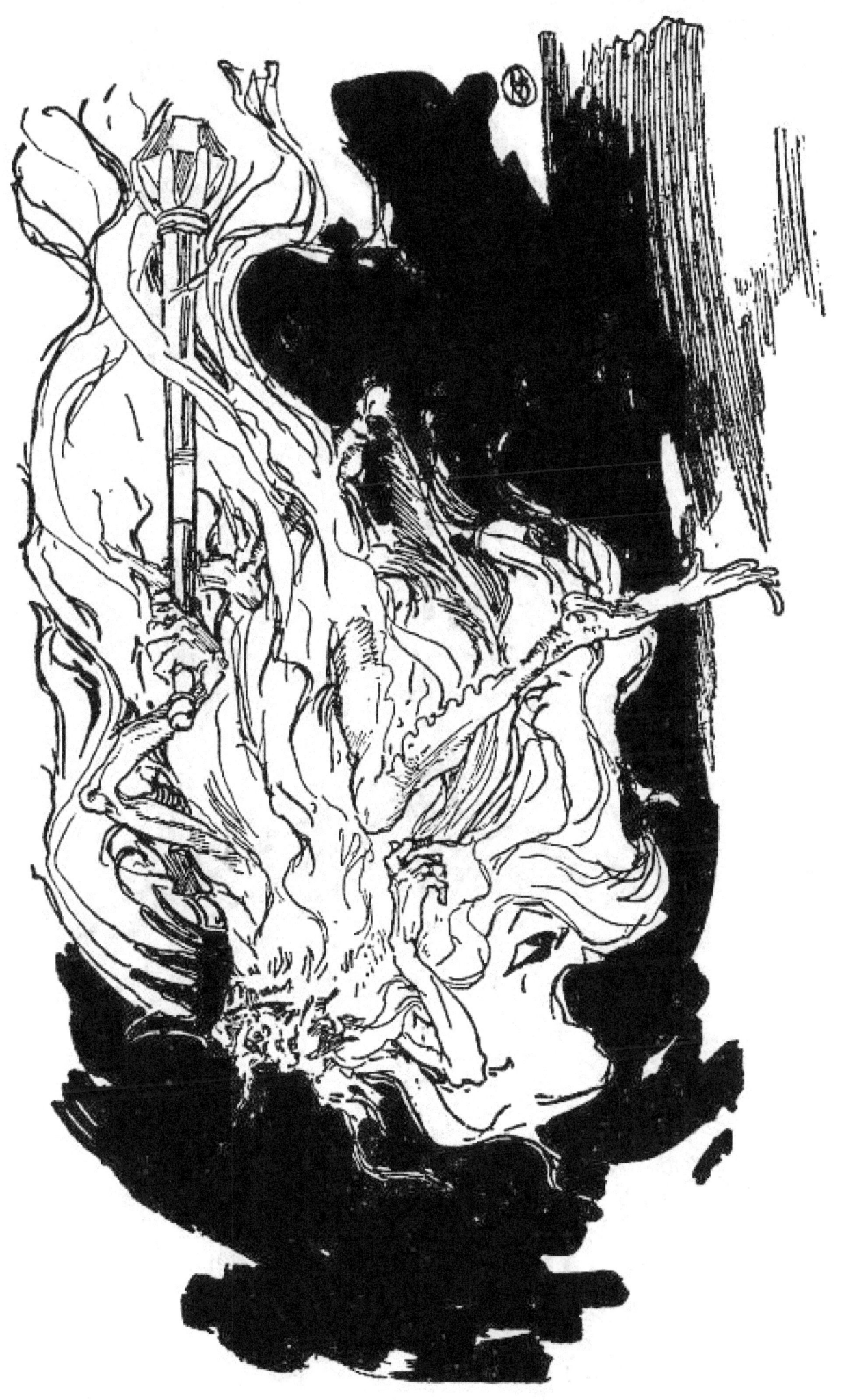

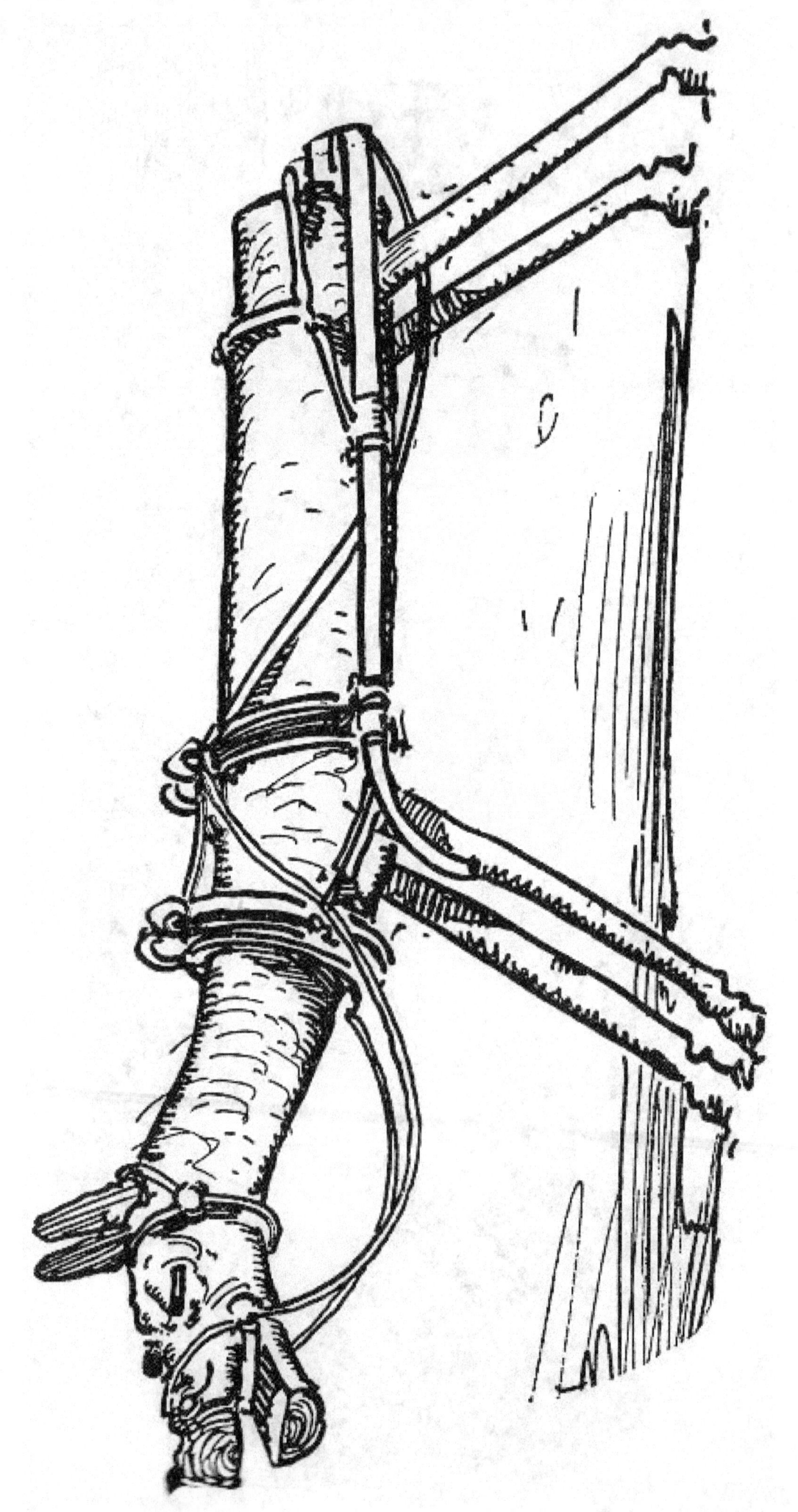

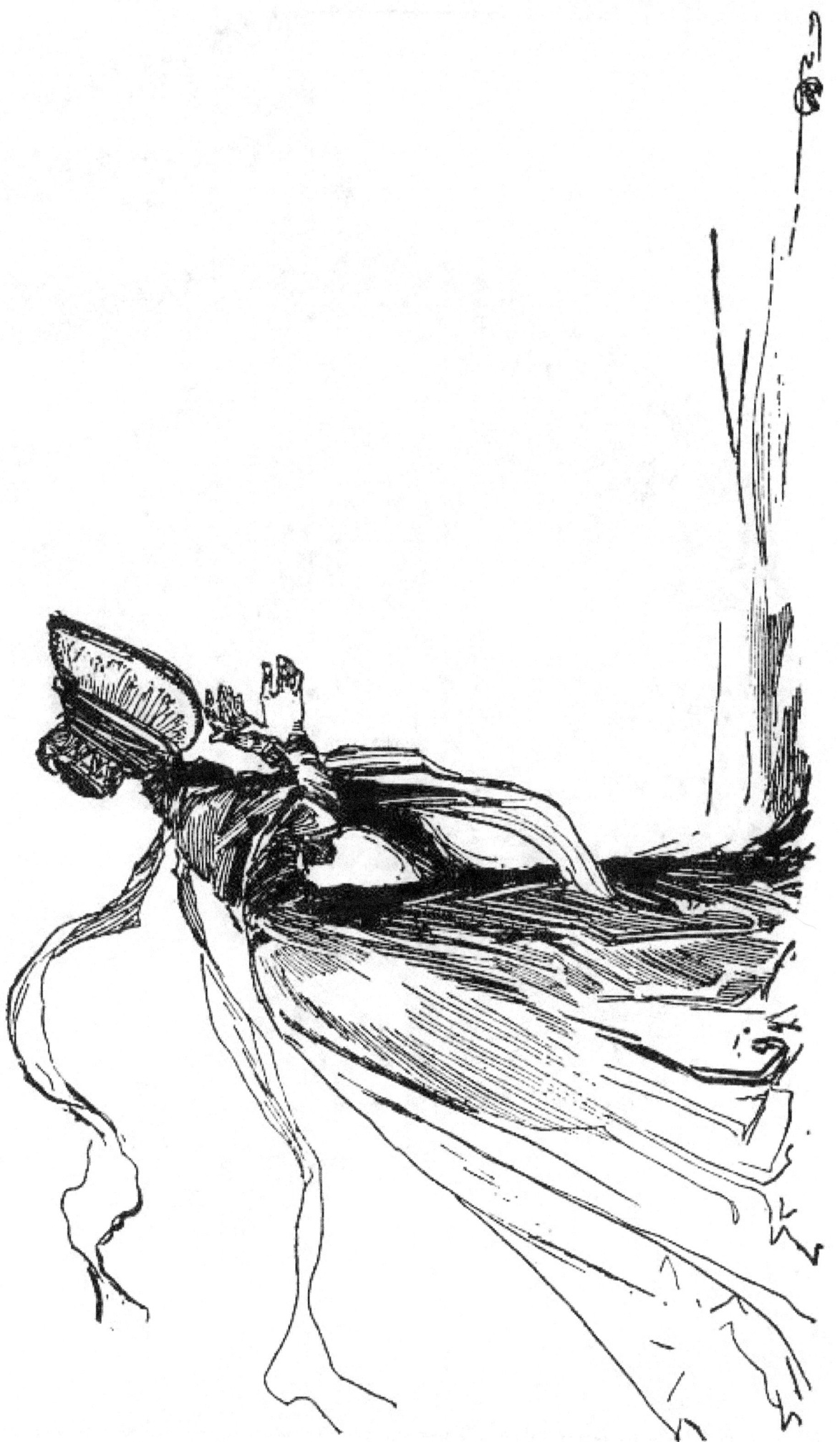

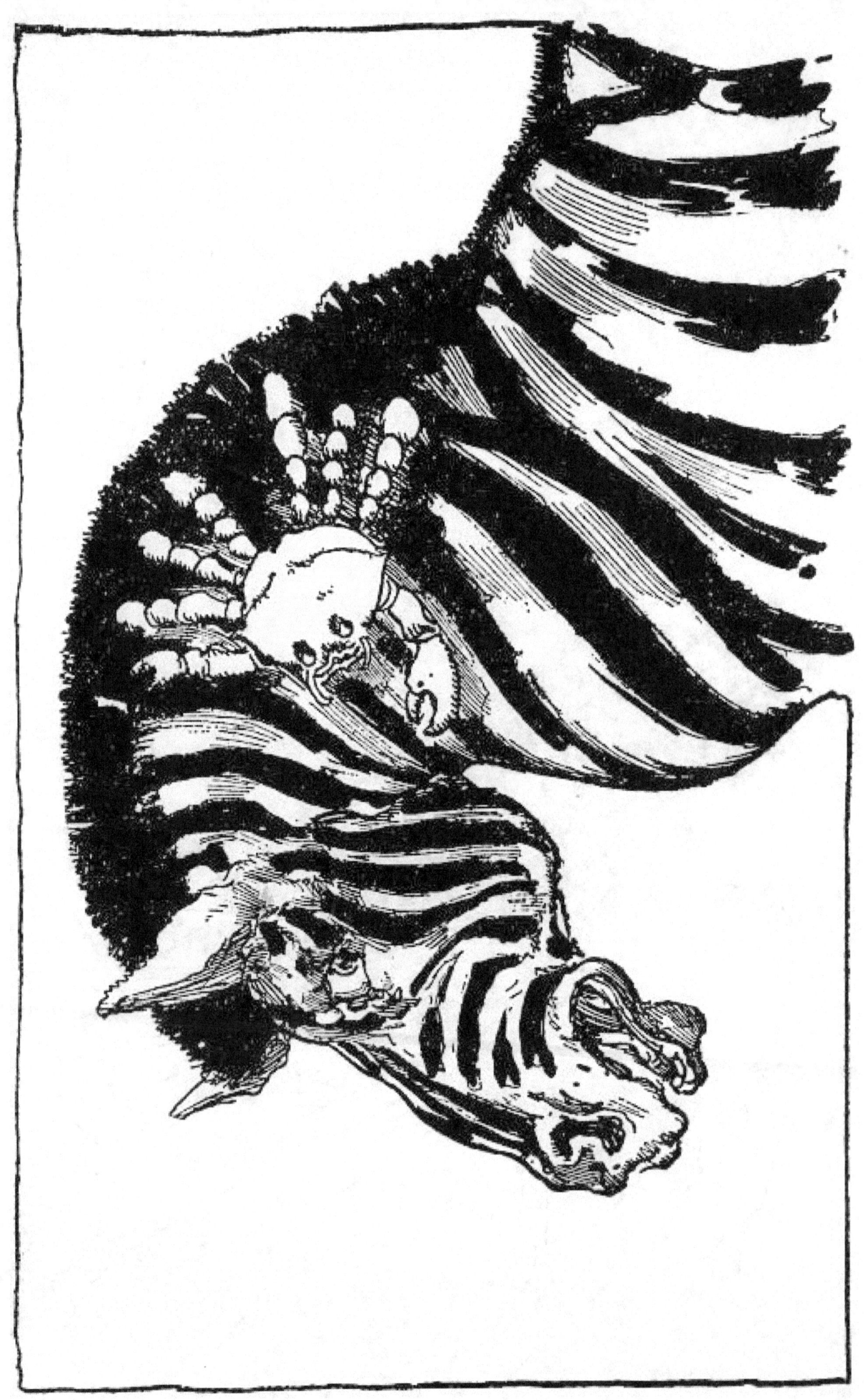

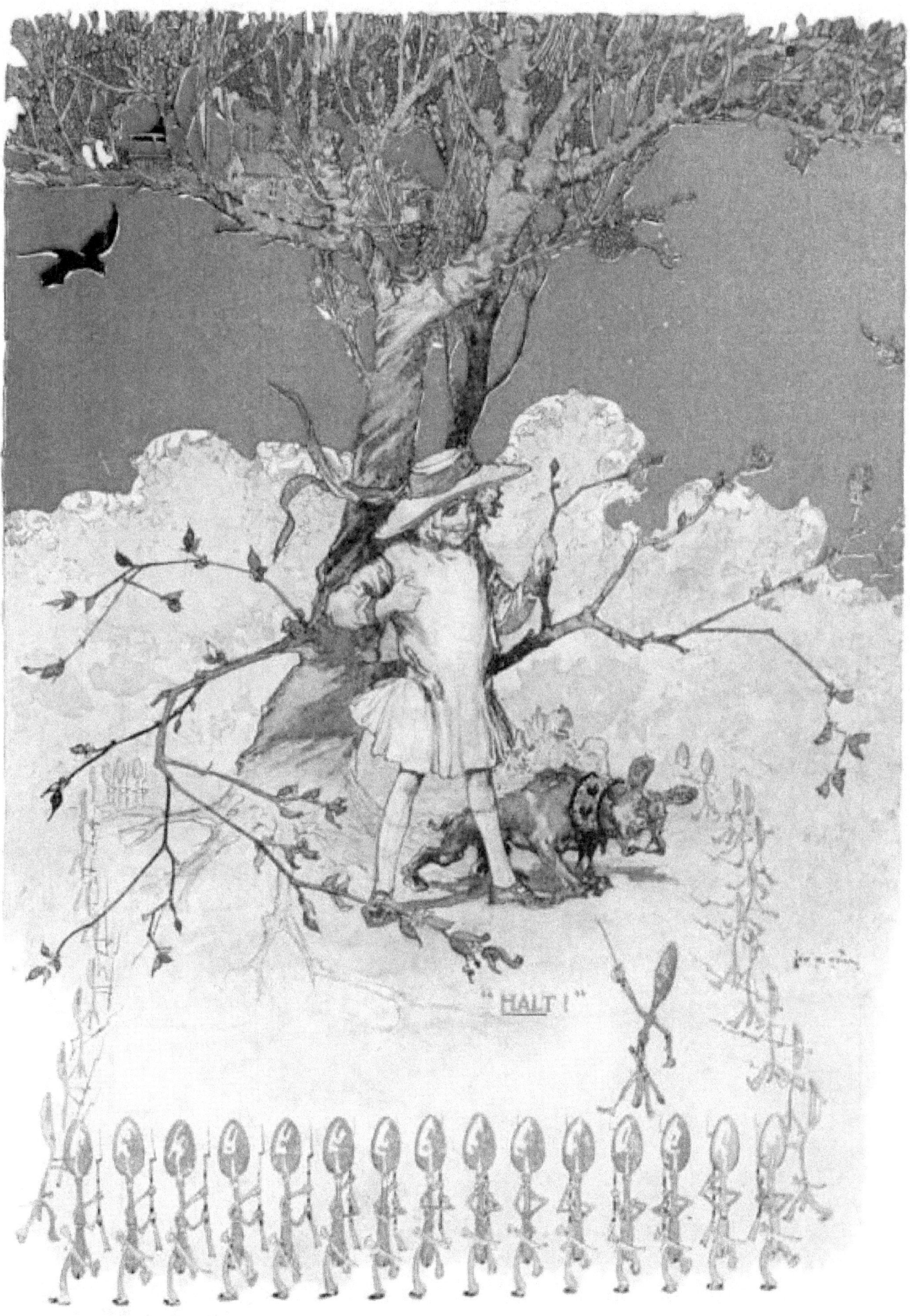

"HALT!"

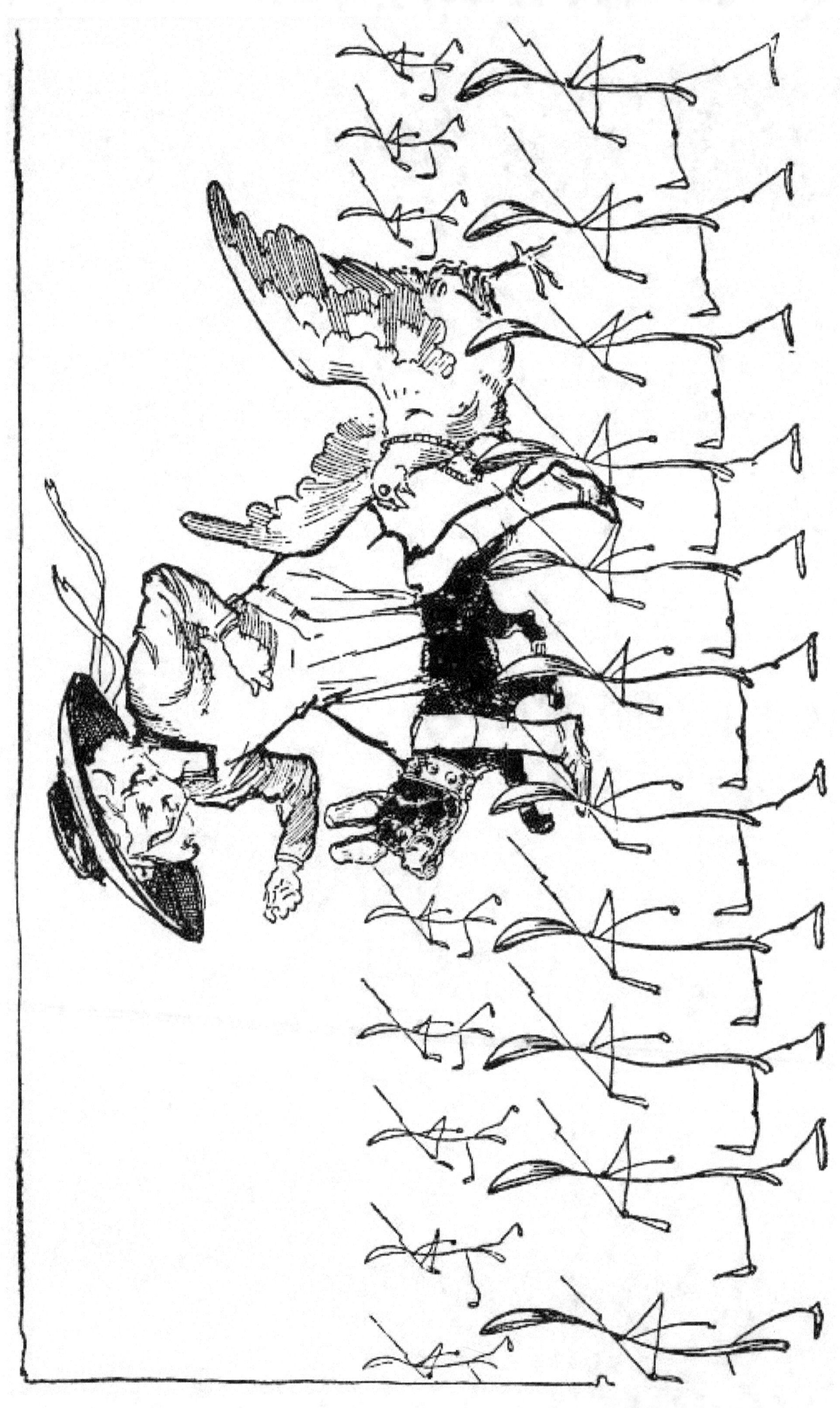

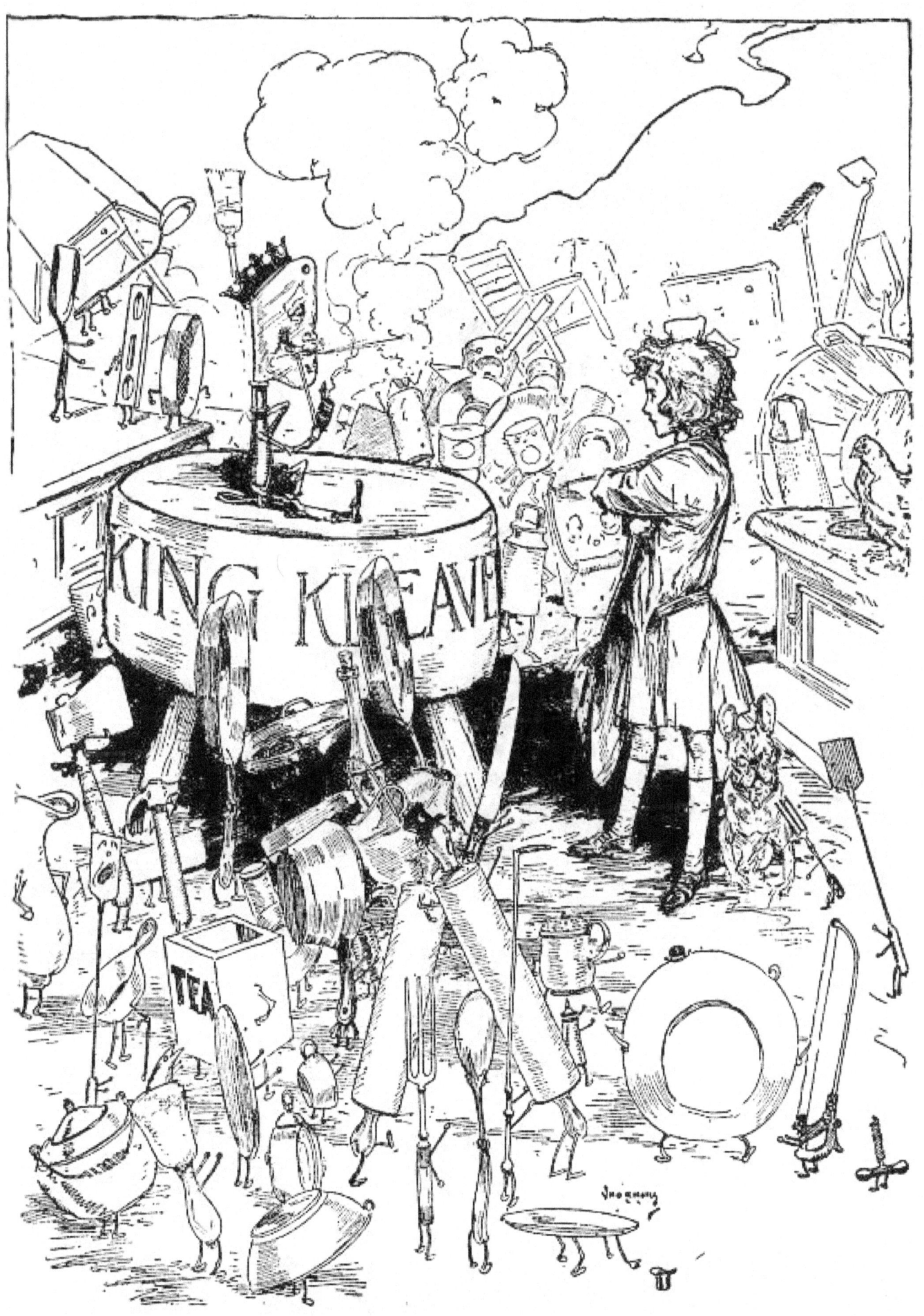

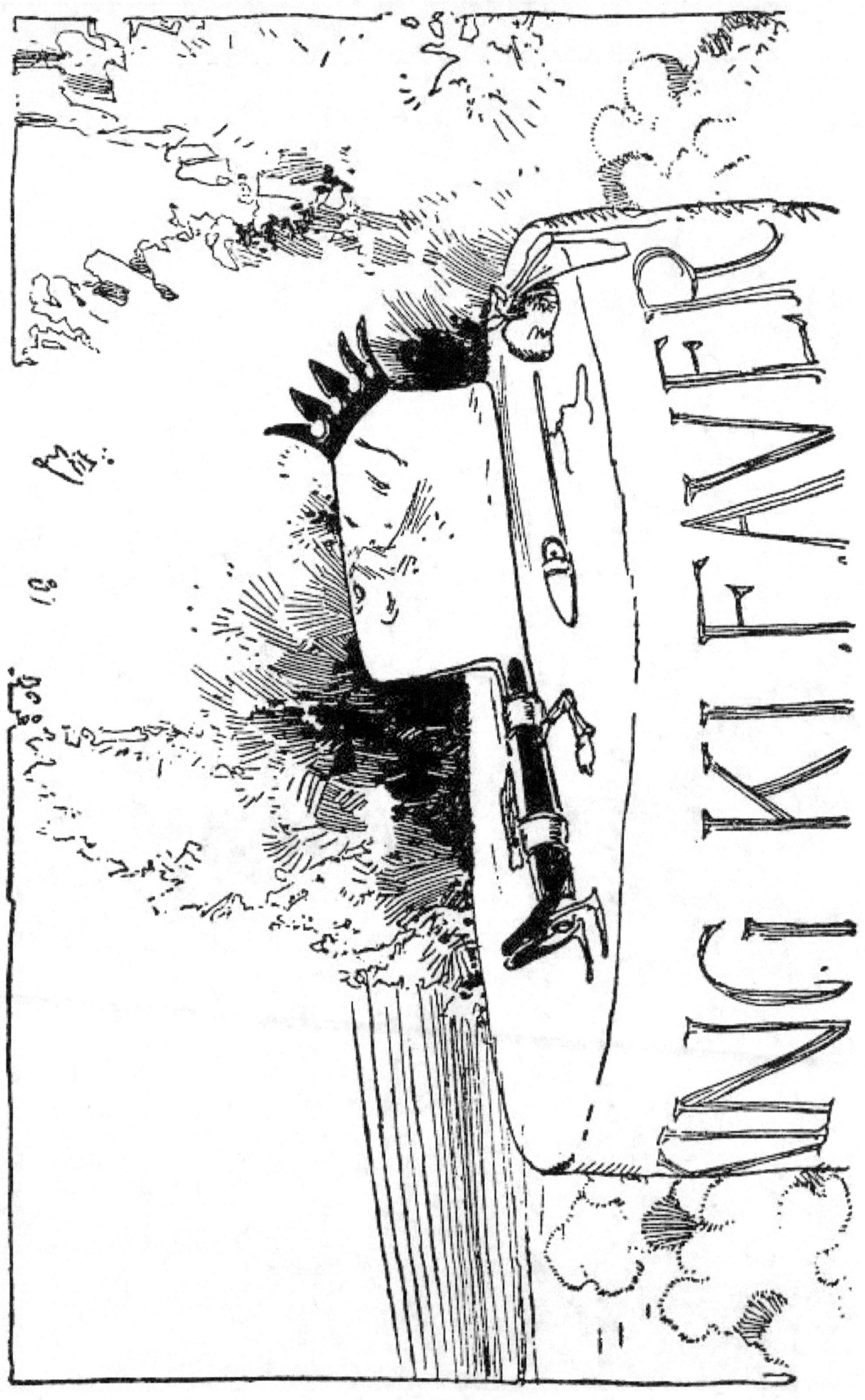

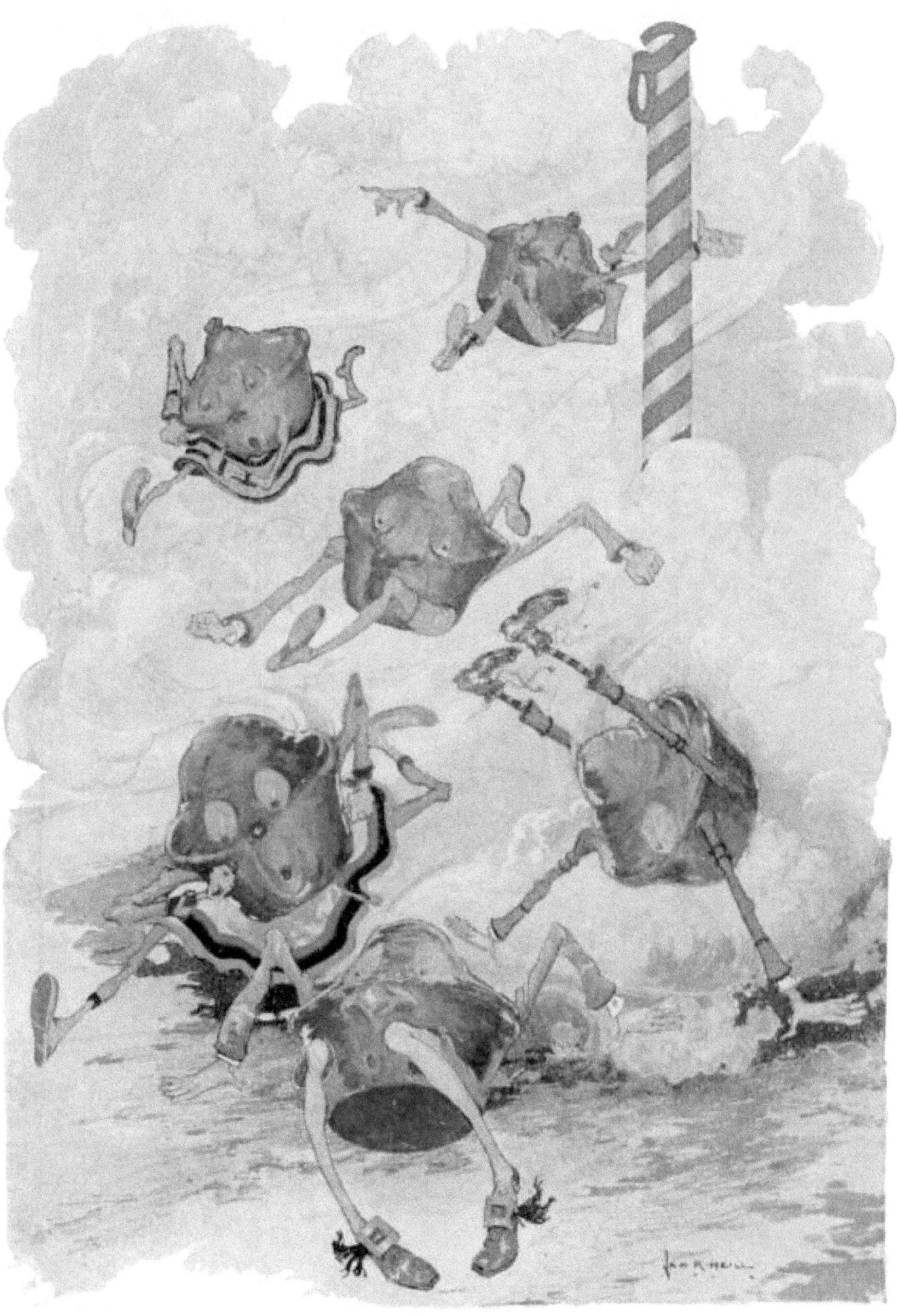

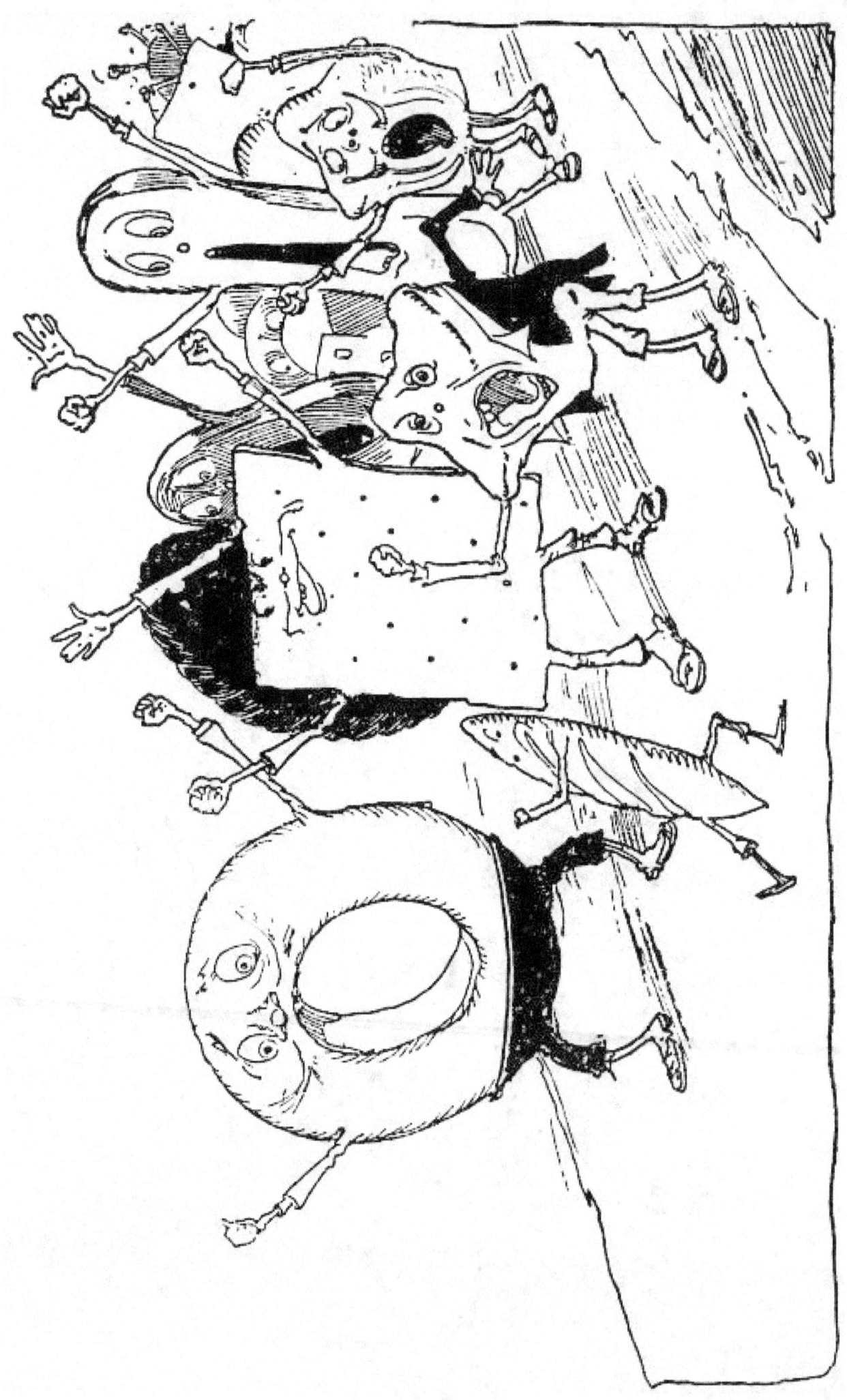

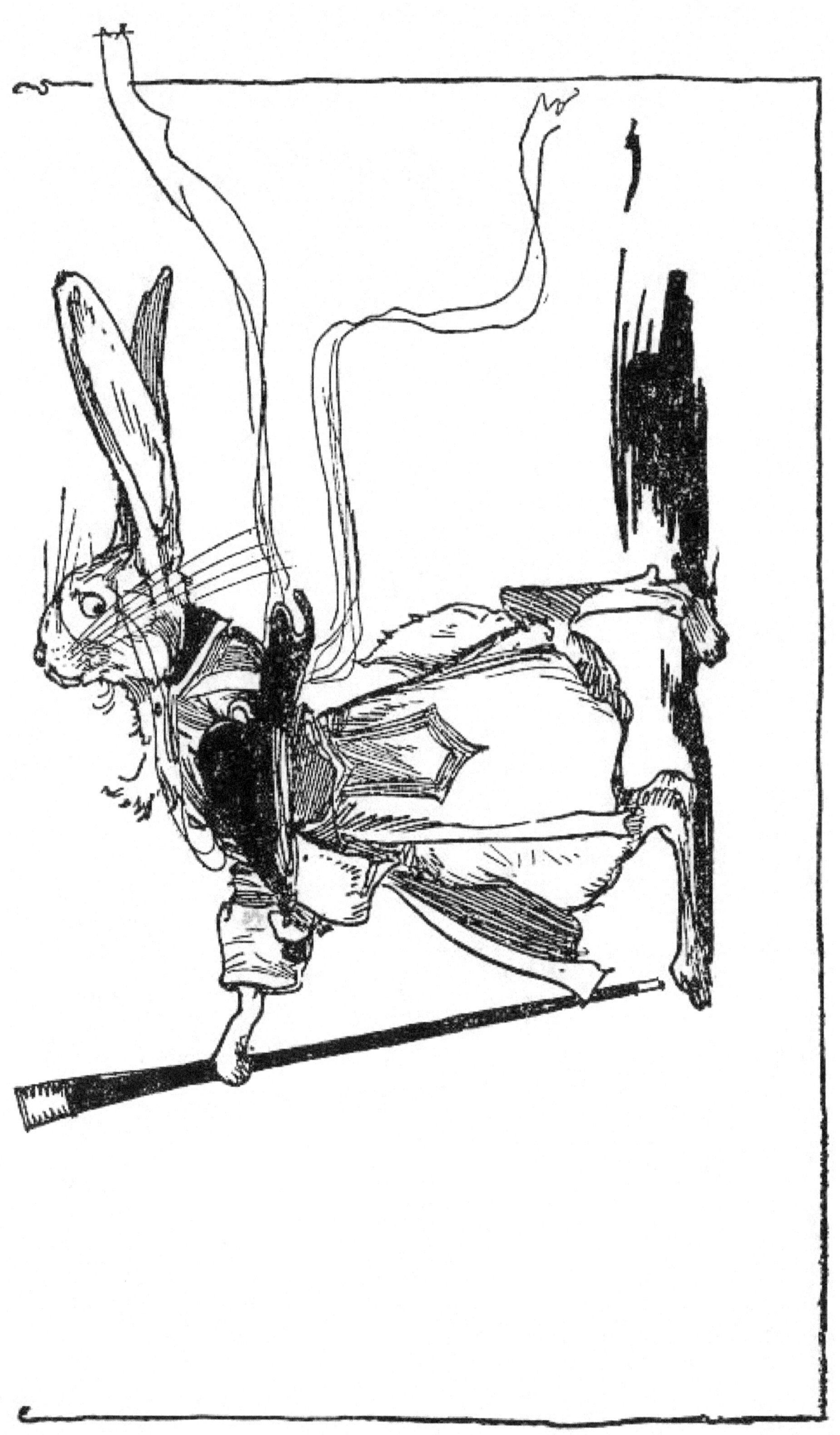

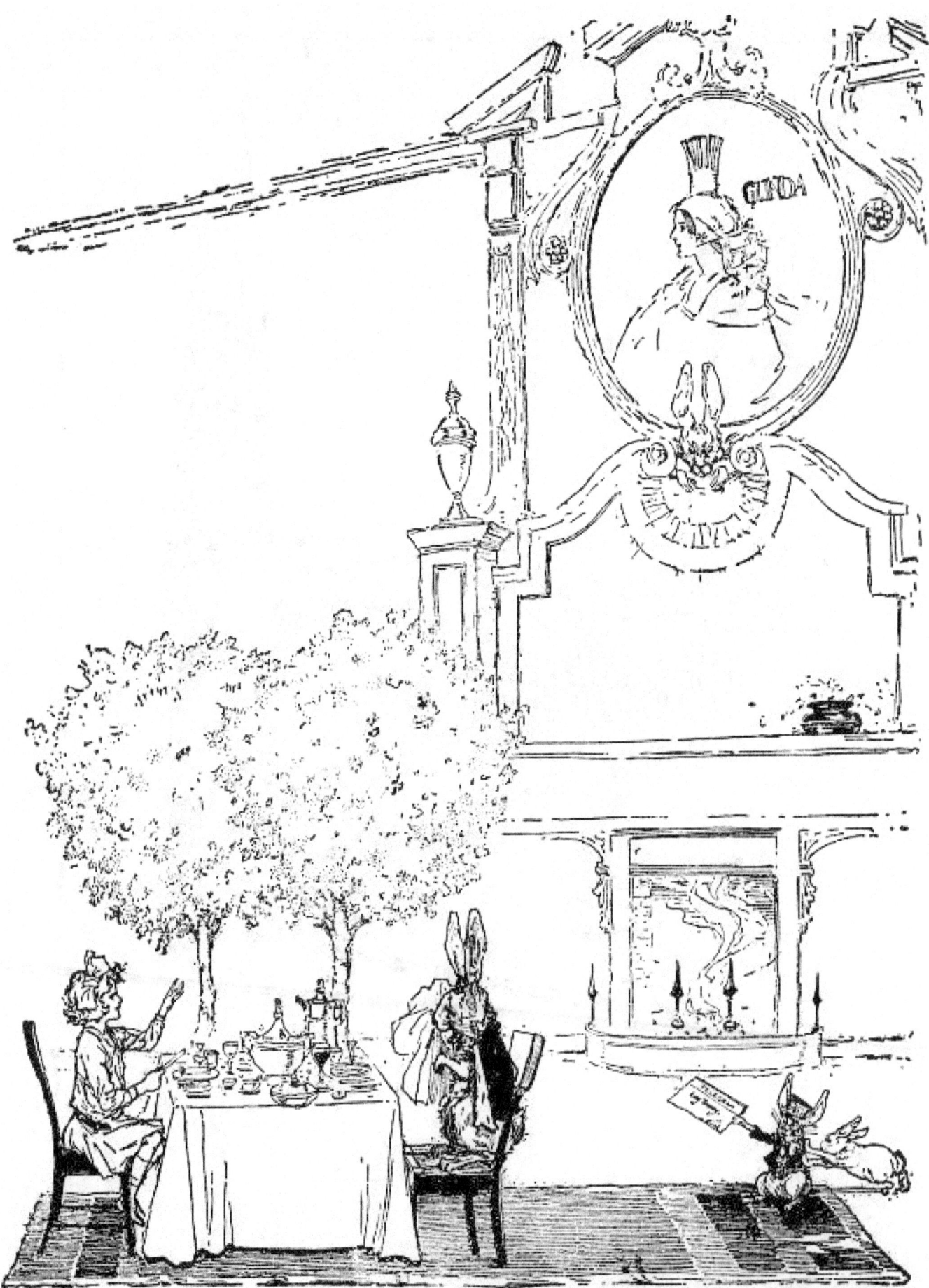

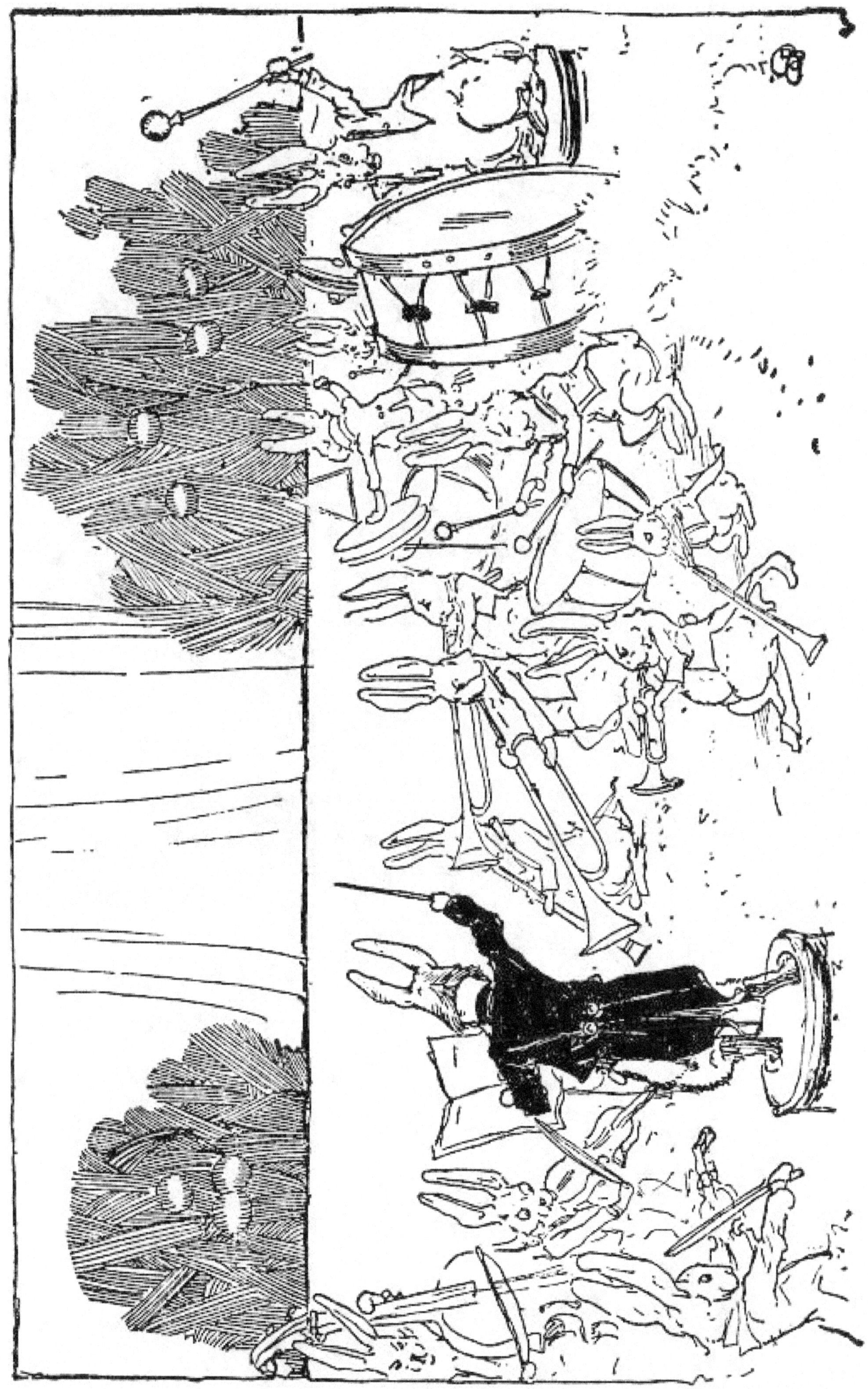

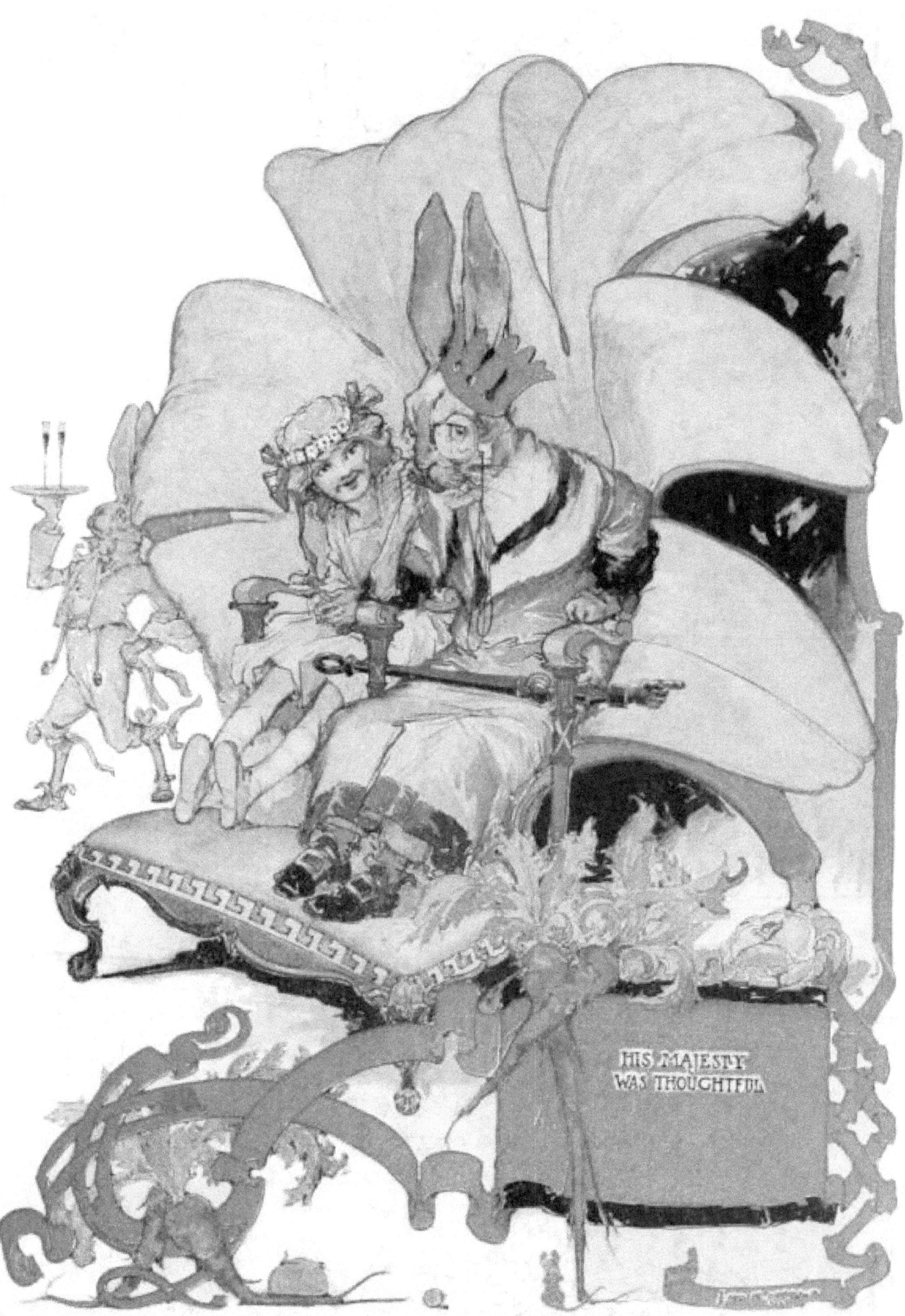

HIS MAJESTY
WAS THOUGHTFUL

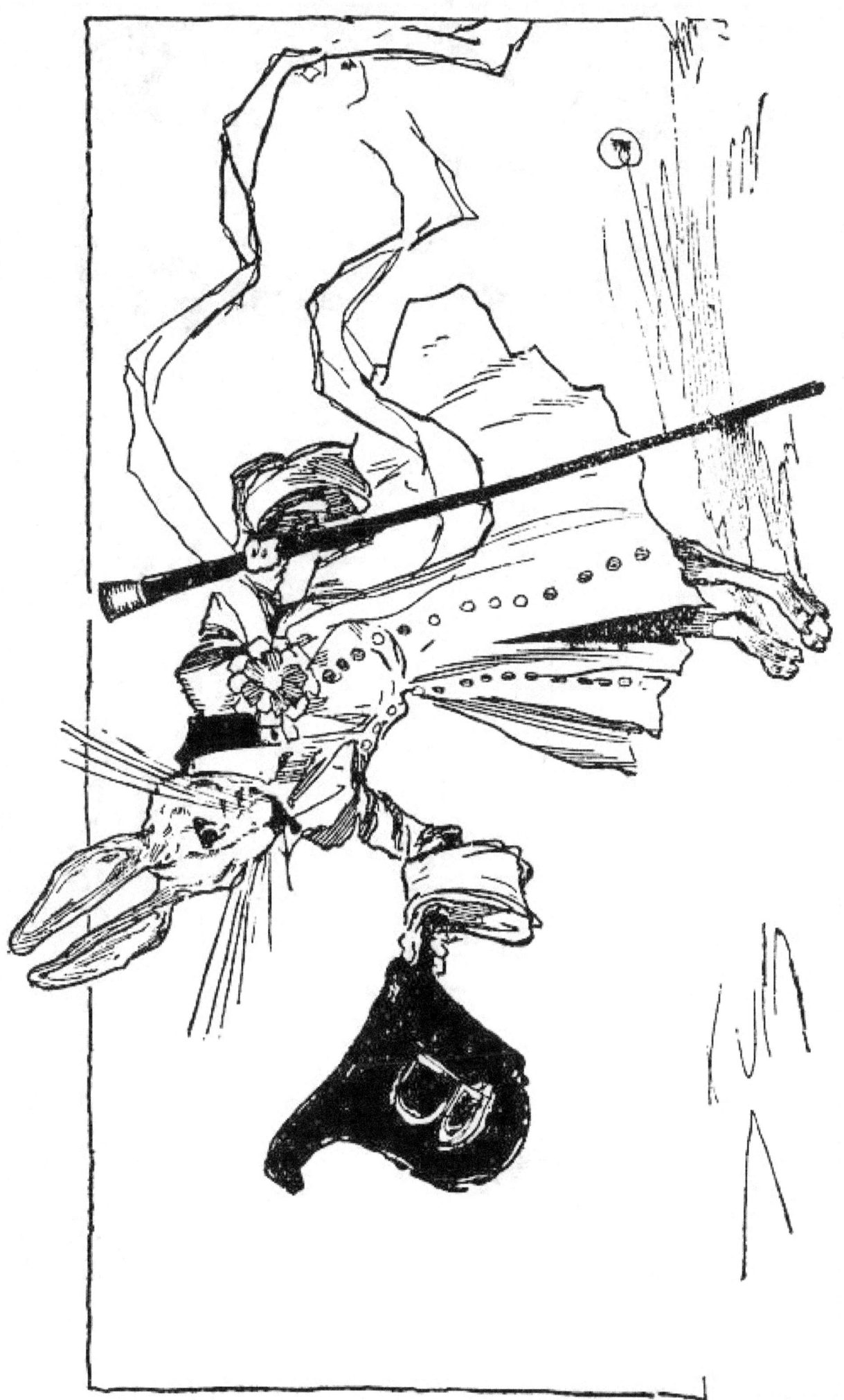

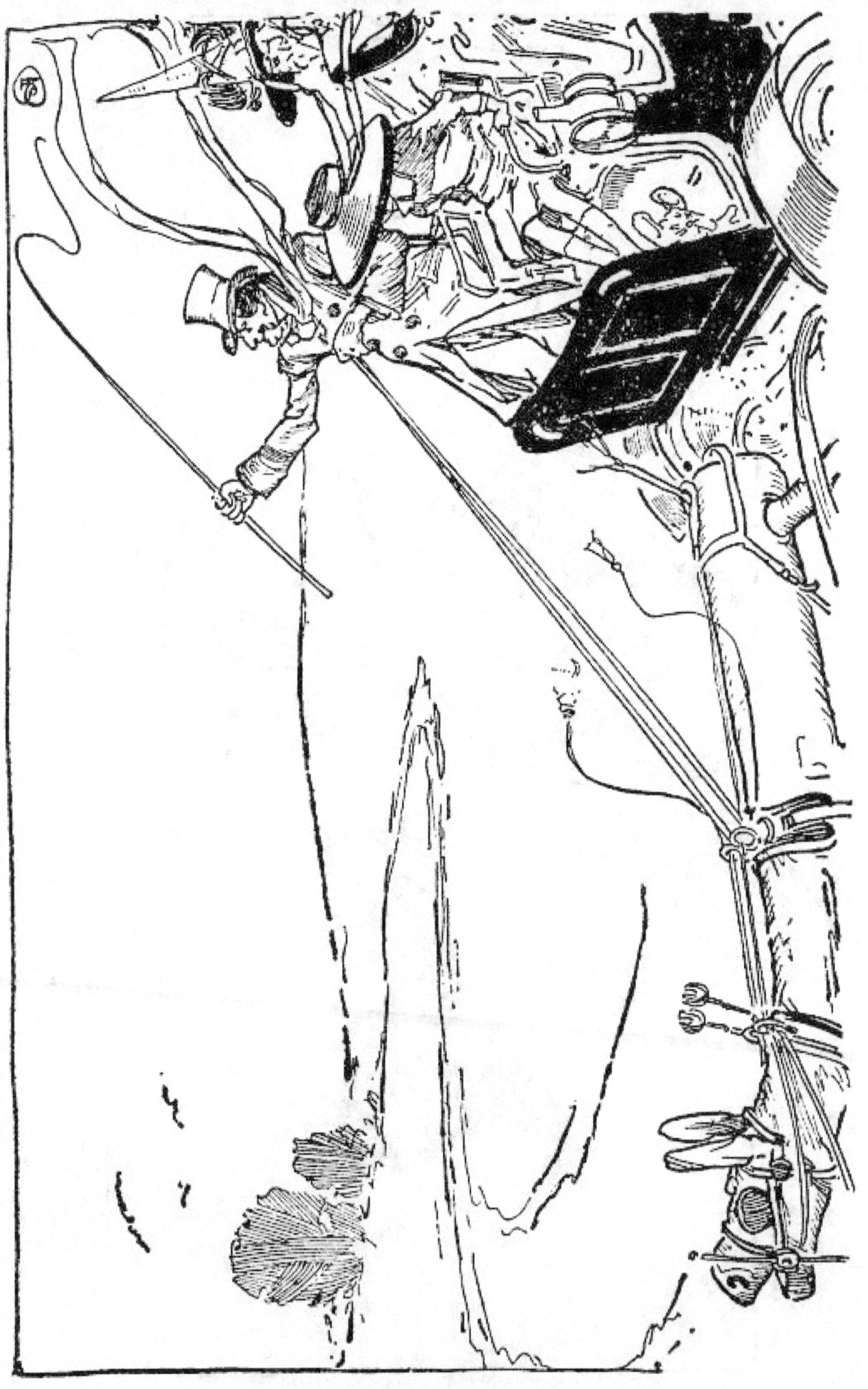

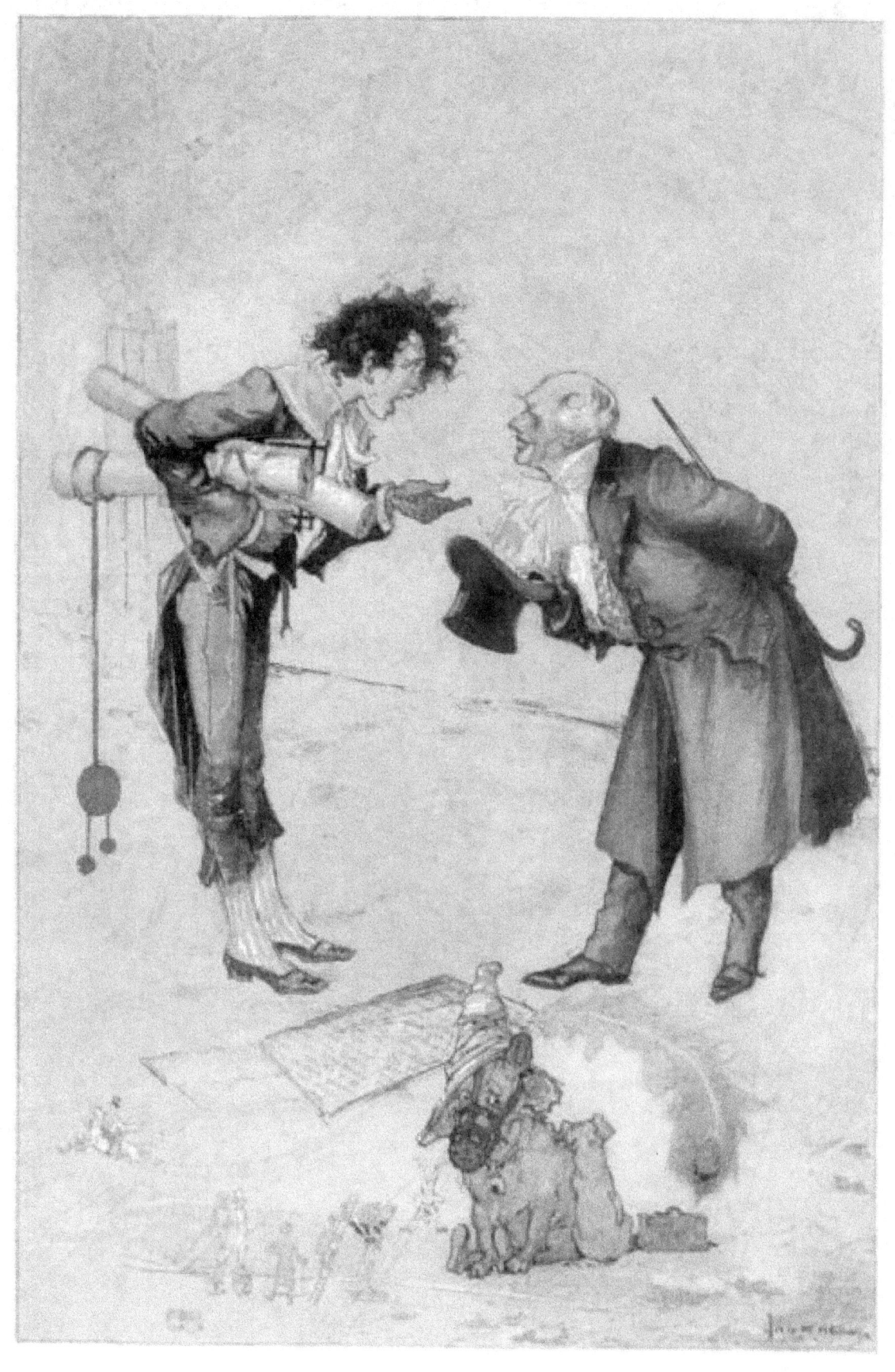

SOANDSO, AND SOANDSO, OH YES, I DON'T KNOW IT MIGHT BE SO I CALCULATE BUT I DON'T KNOW, IN TRE MINTRY CUTEYCORN APPLE SEEDS AND FLY AWAY JACK • SIX SIXES ARE NOT SIXTY – SIX ? AND WE STILL HOLD TO FOLDEROL DE DOODLE ALL DAY, IF I HAD A DONKEY THAT WOULD'NT GO I'D BUY A FIDDLE FOR FIFTY CENTS AND RATTLE HIS BONES OVER THE STONES IT'S ONLY A BEGGAR WHOM NOBODY OWNS, LISTEN ??

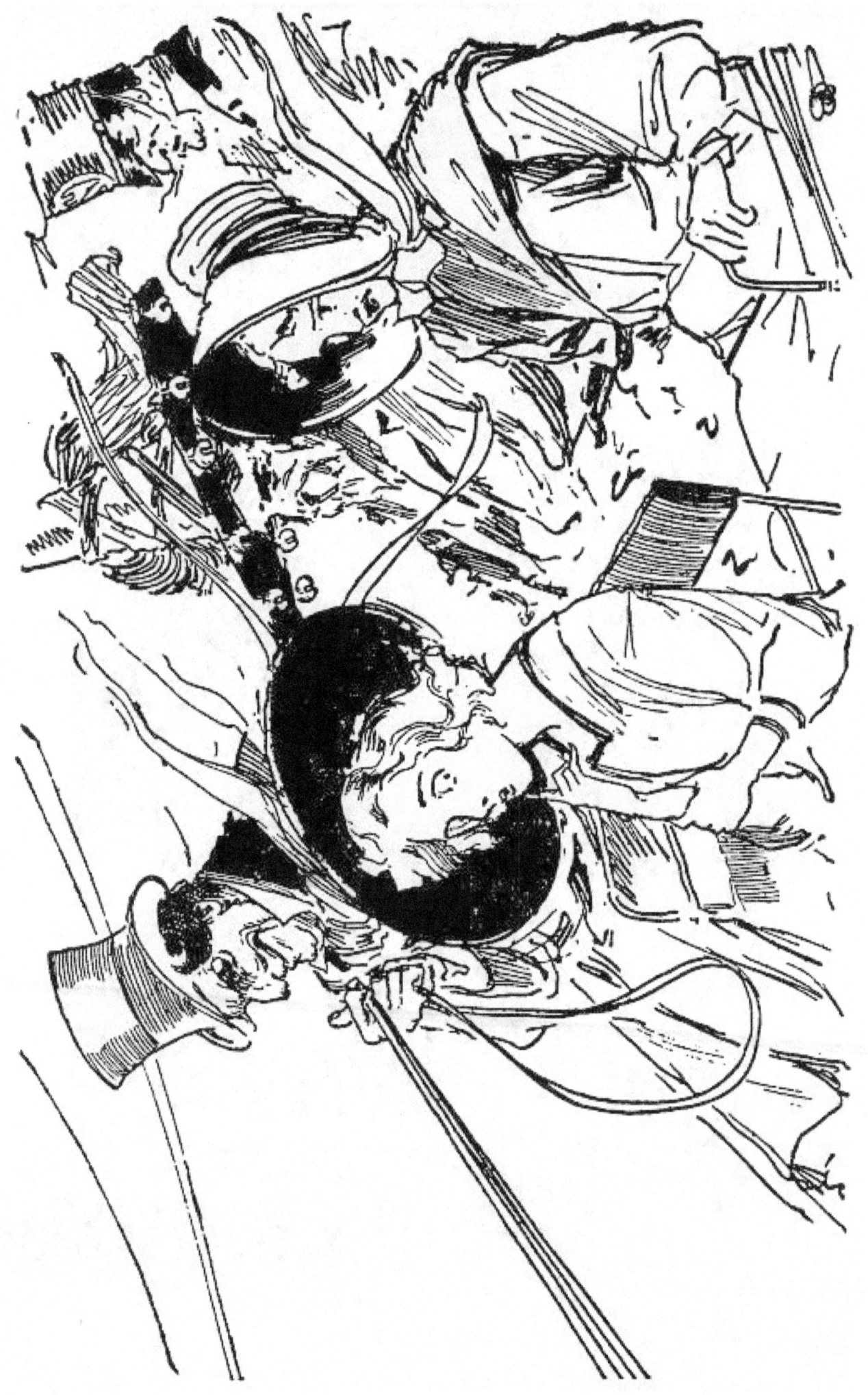

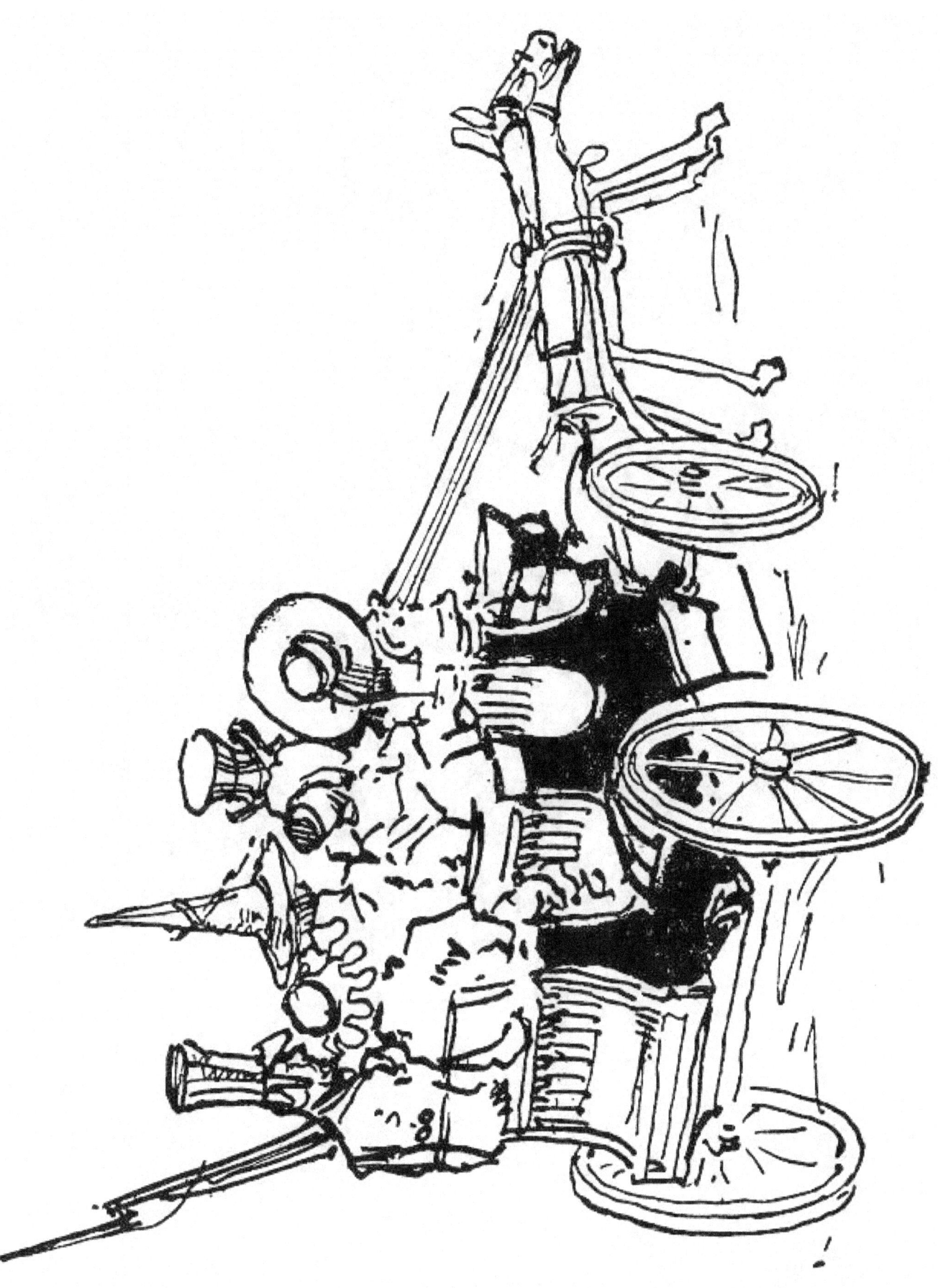

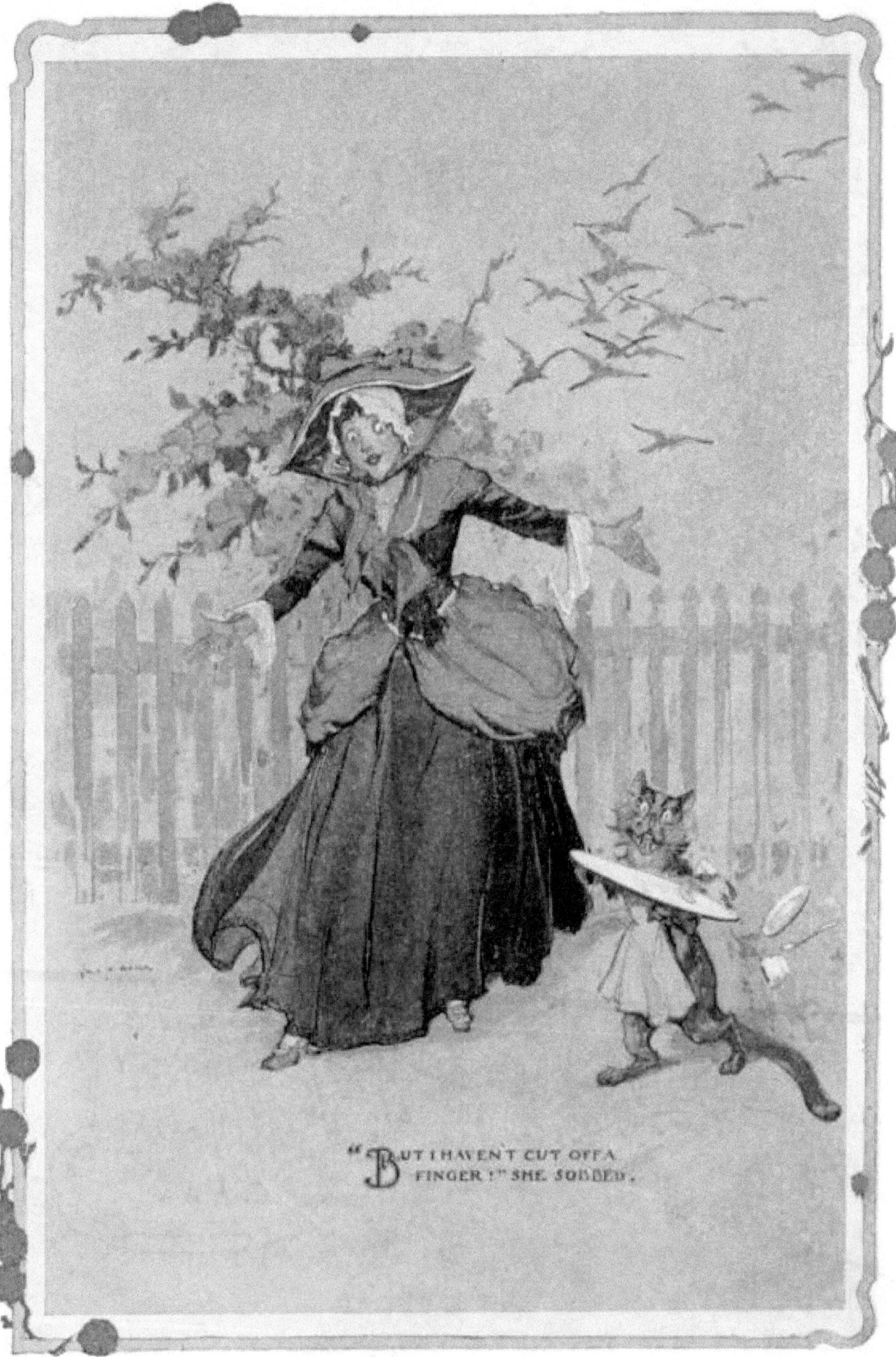

"BUT I HAVEN'T CUT OFF A
FINGER!" SHE SOBBED.

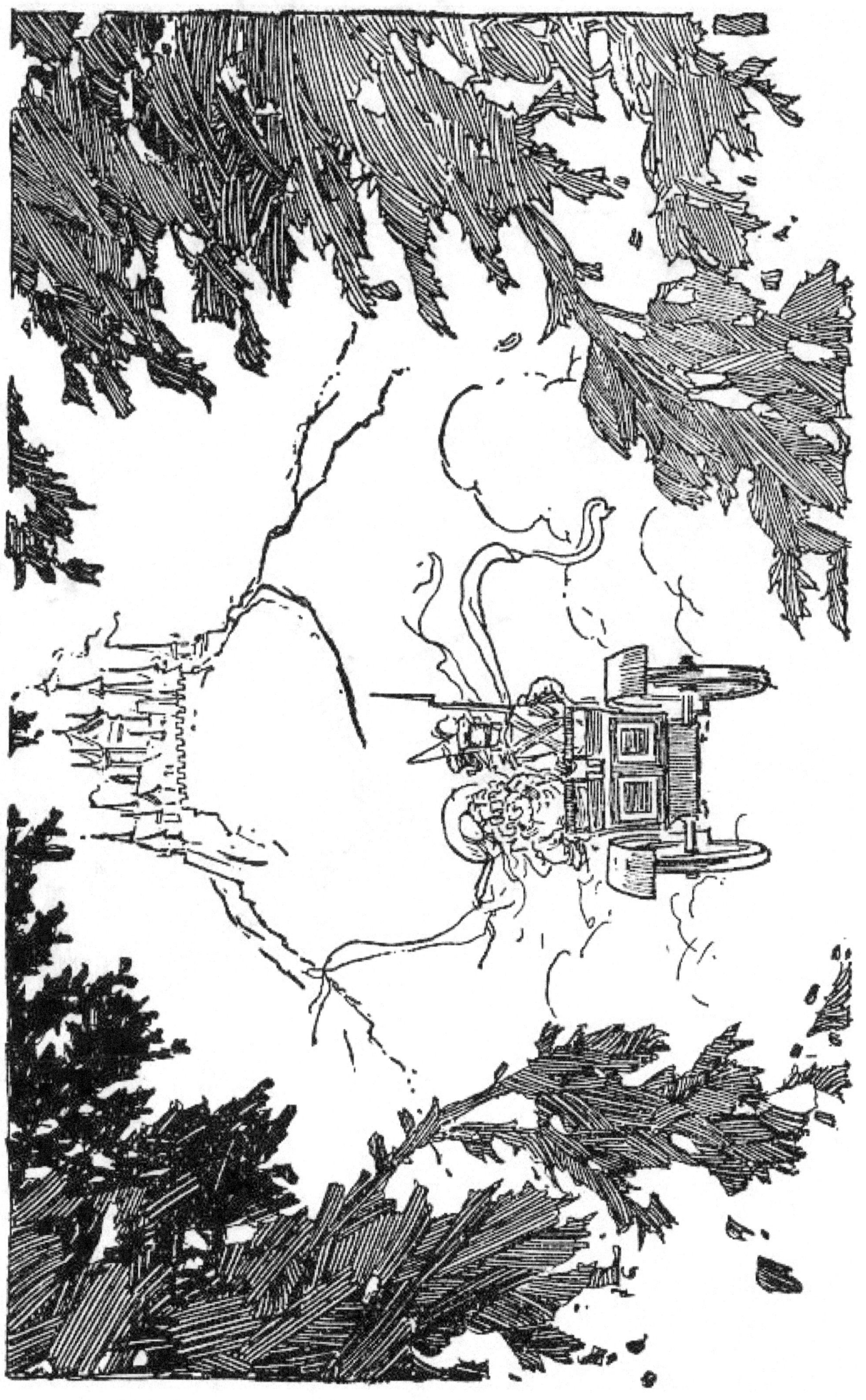

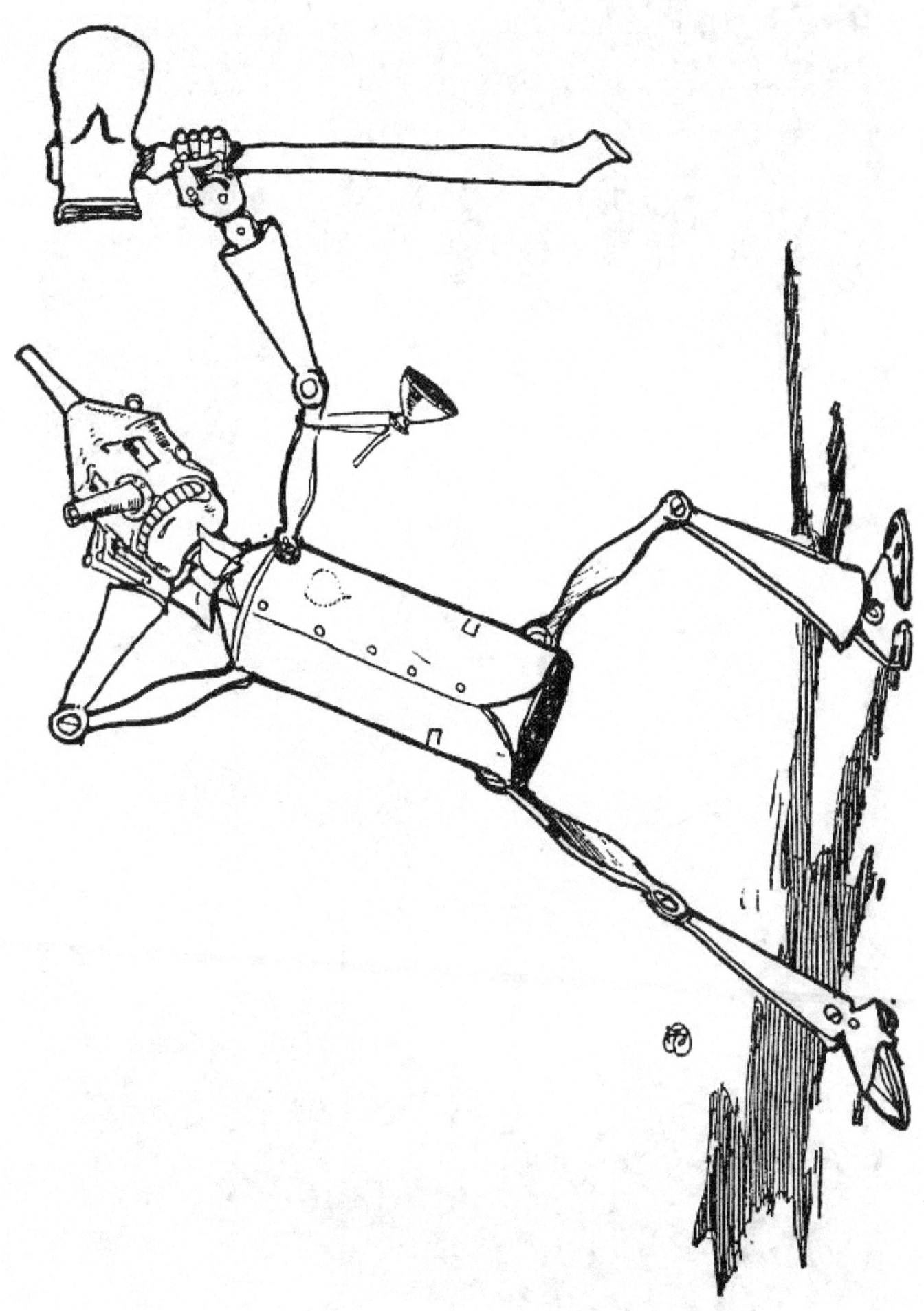

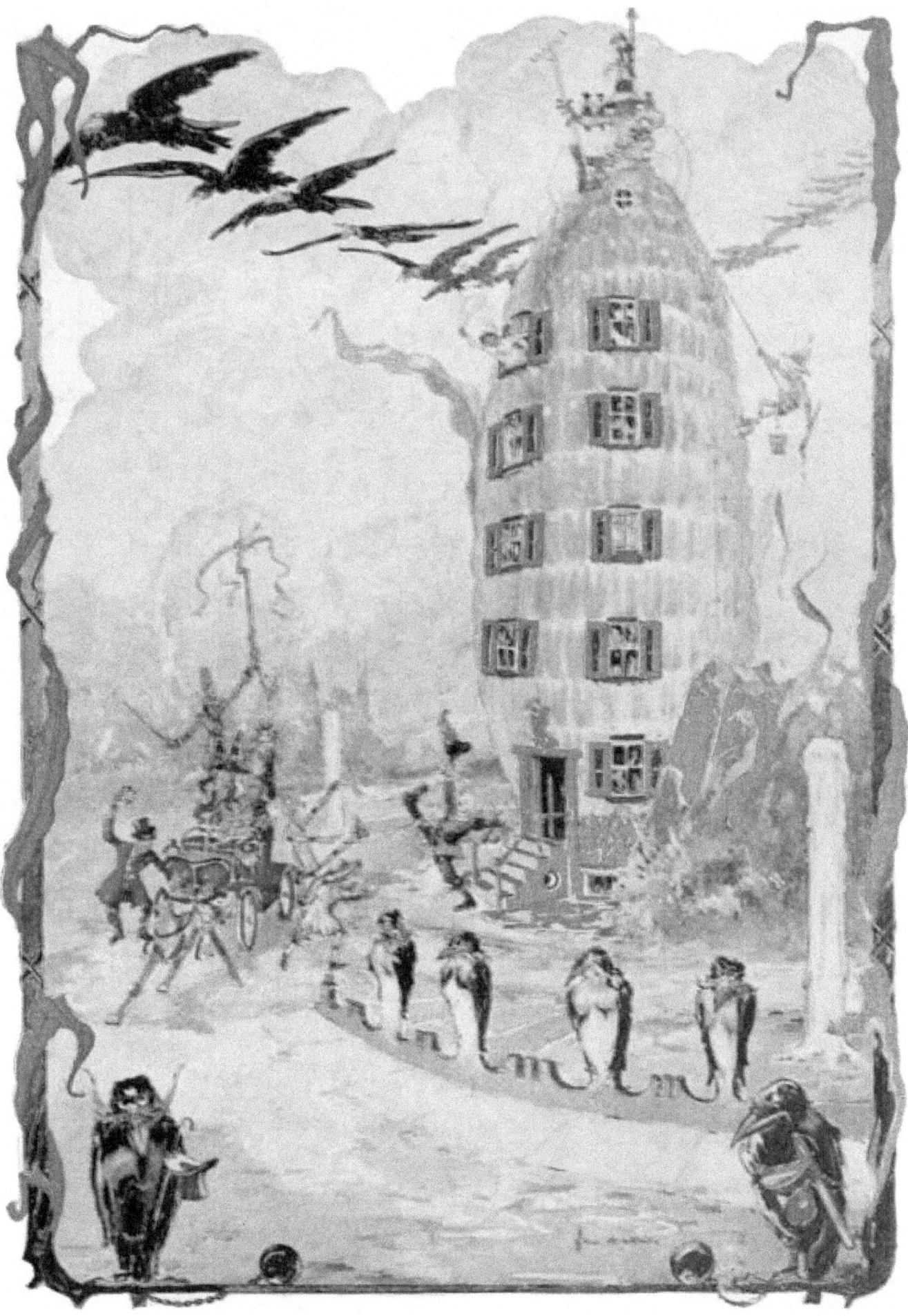

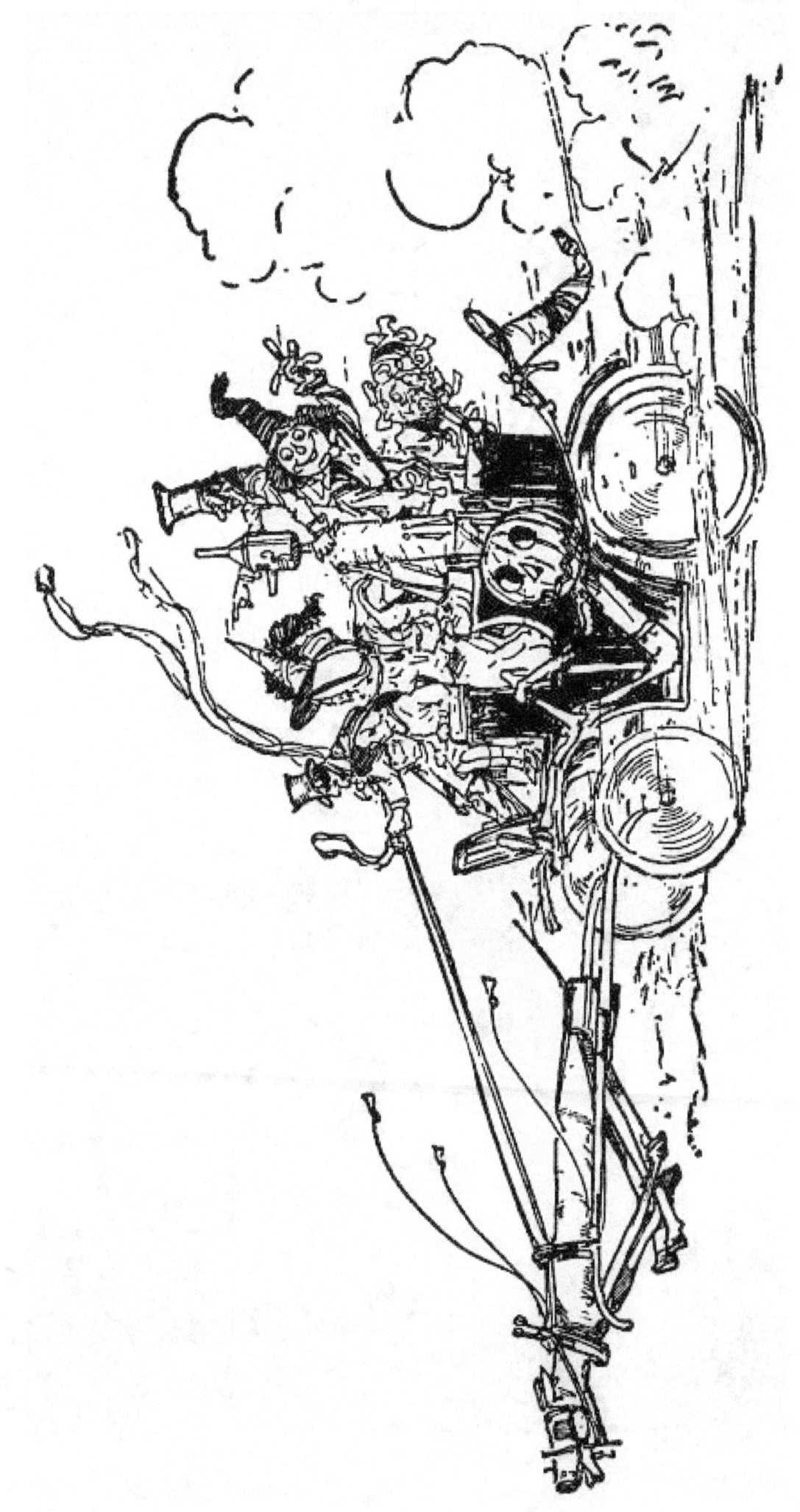

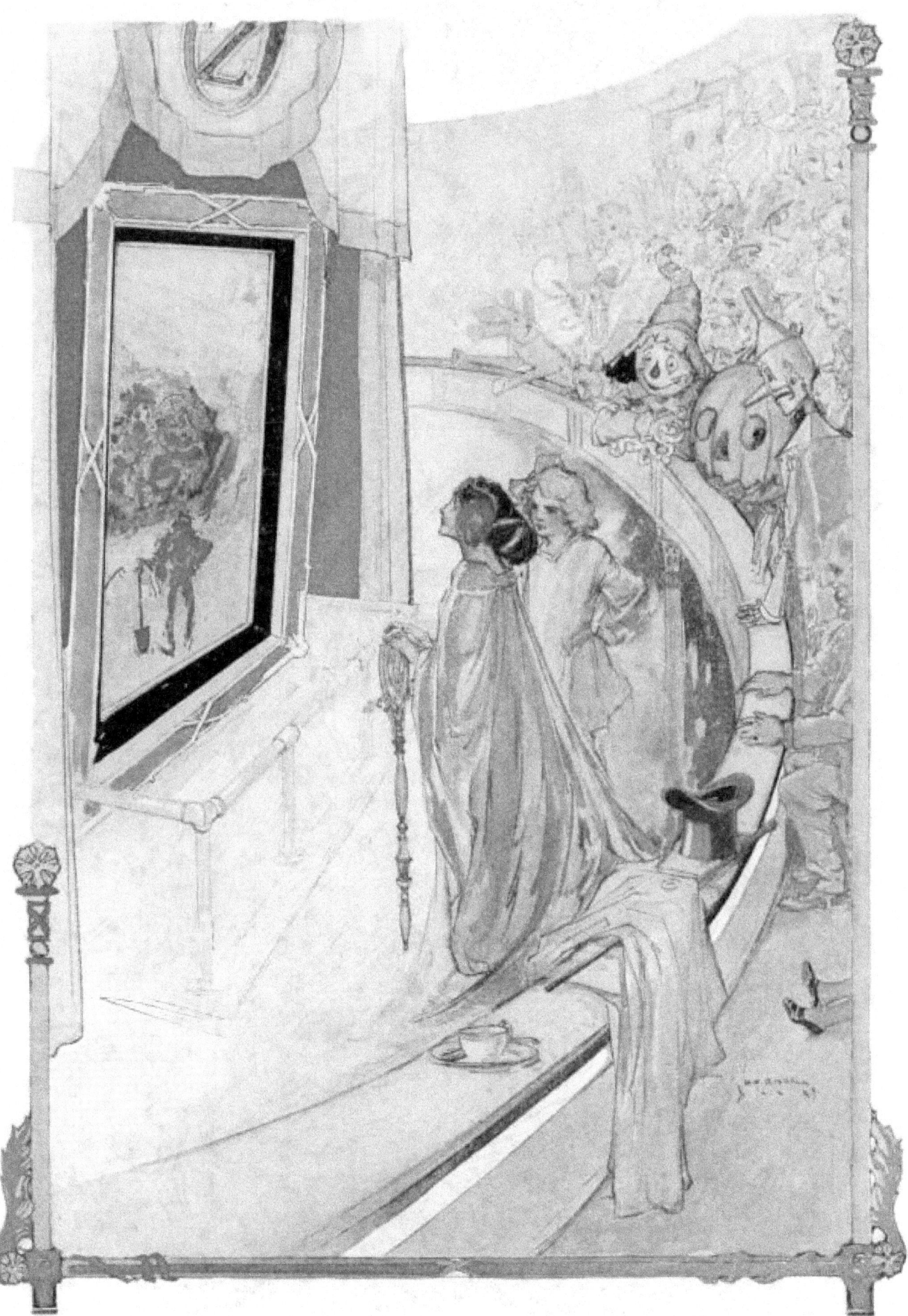

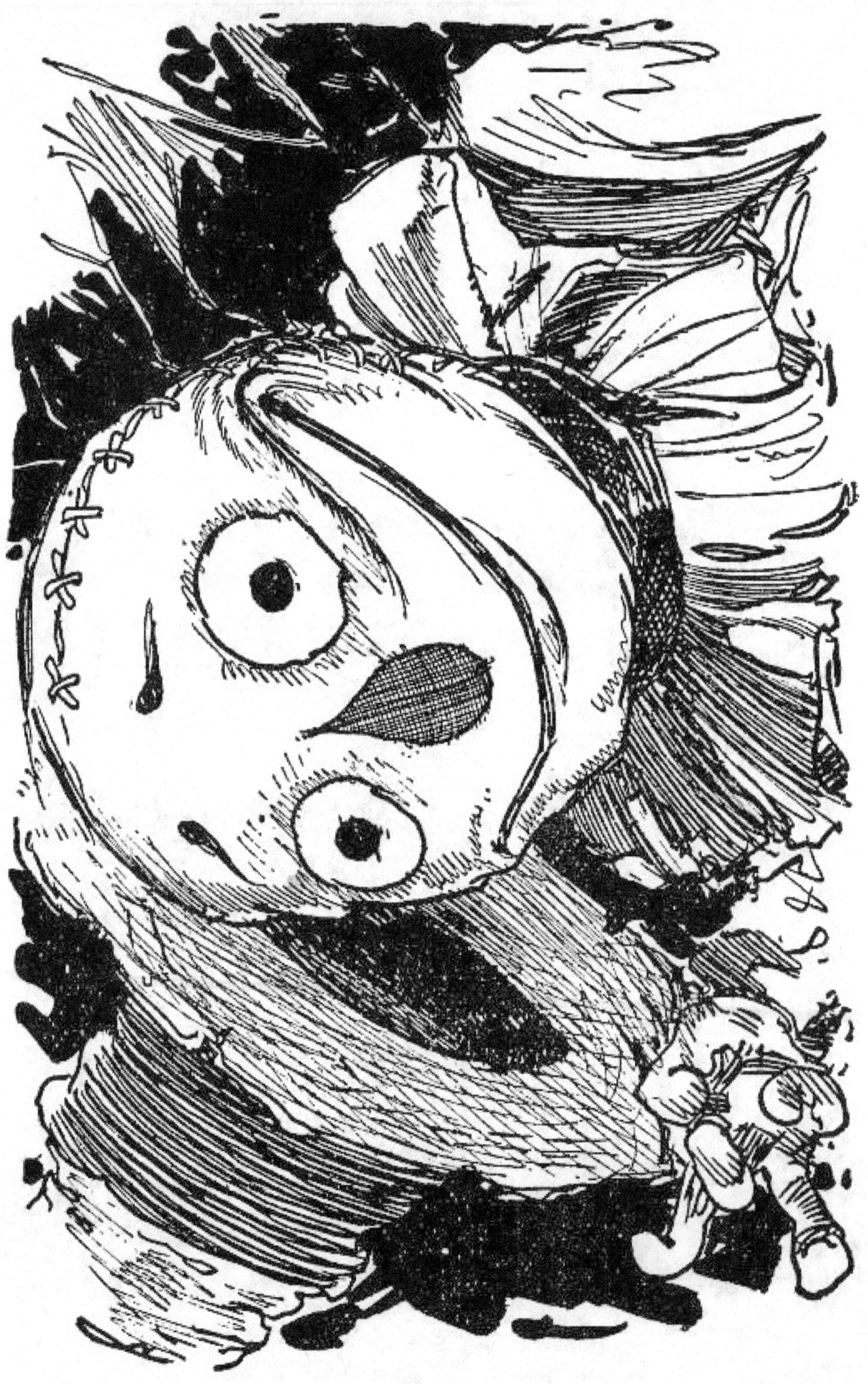

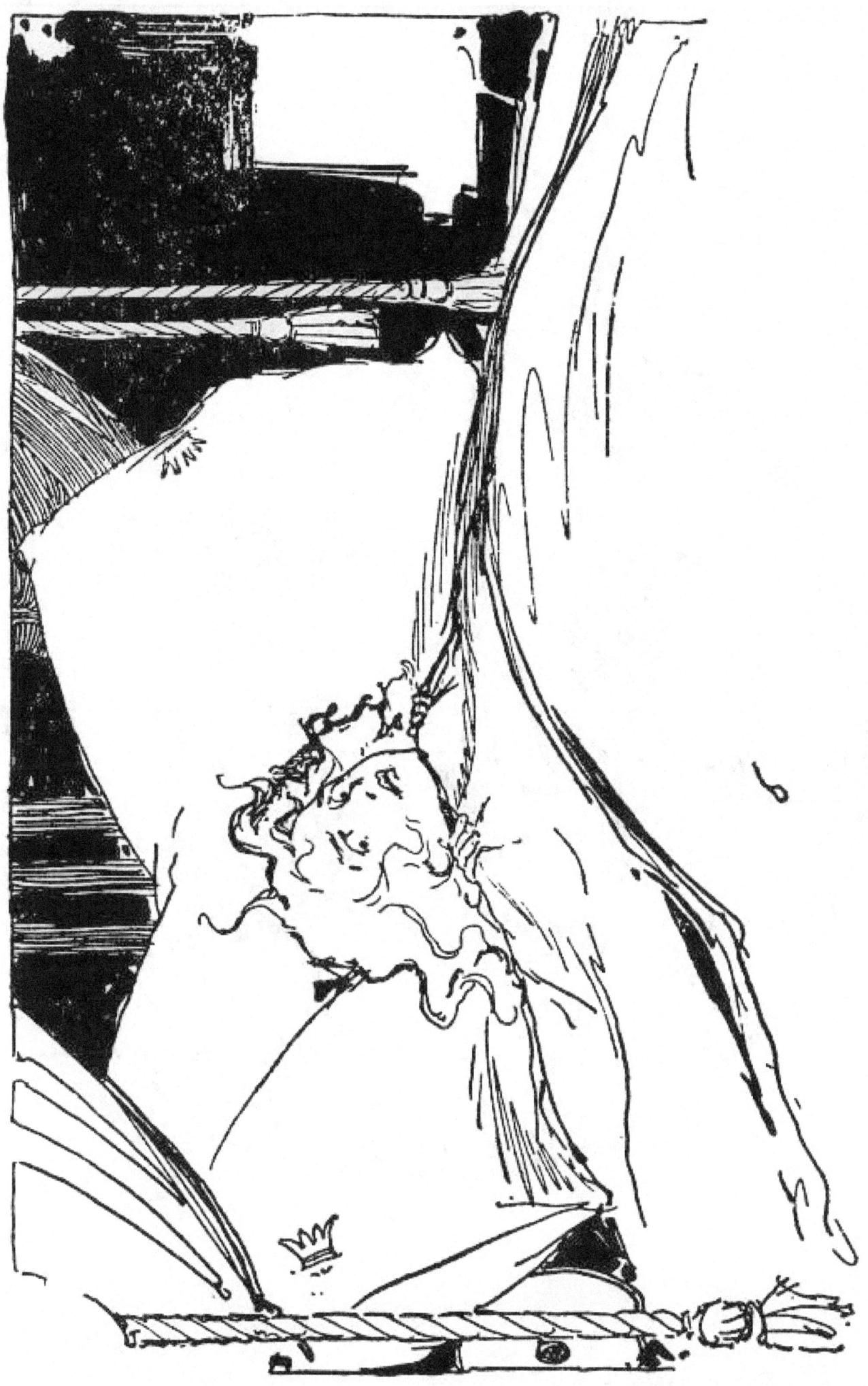

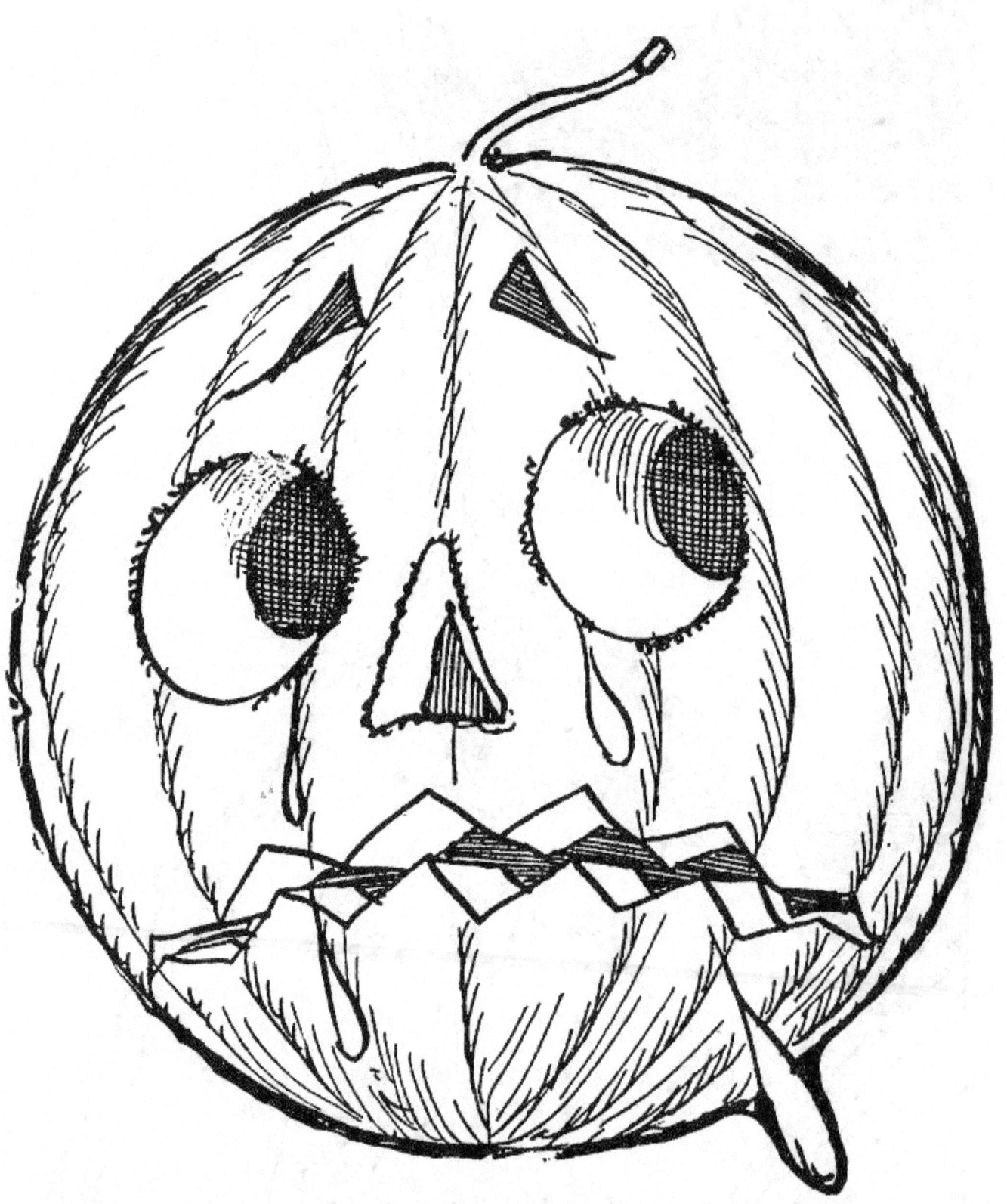

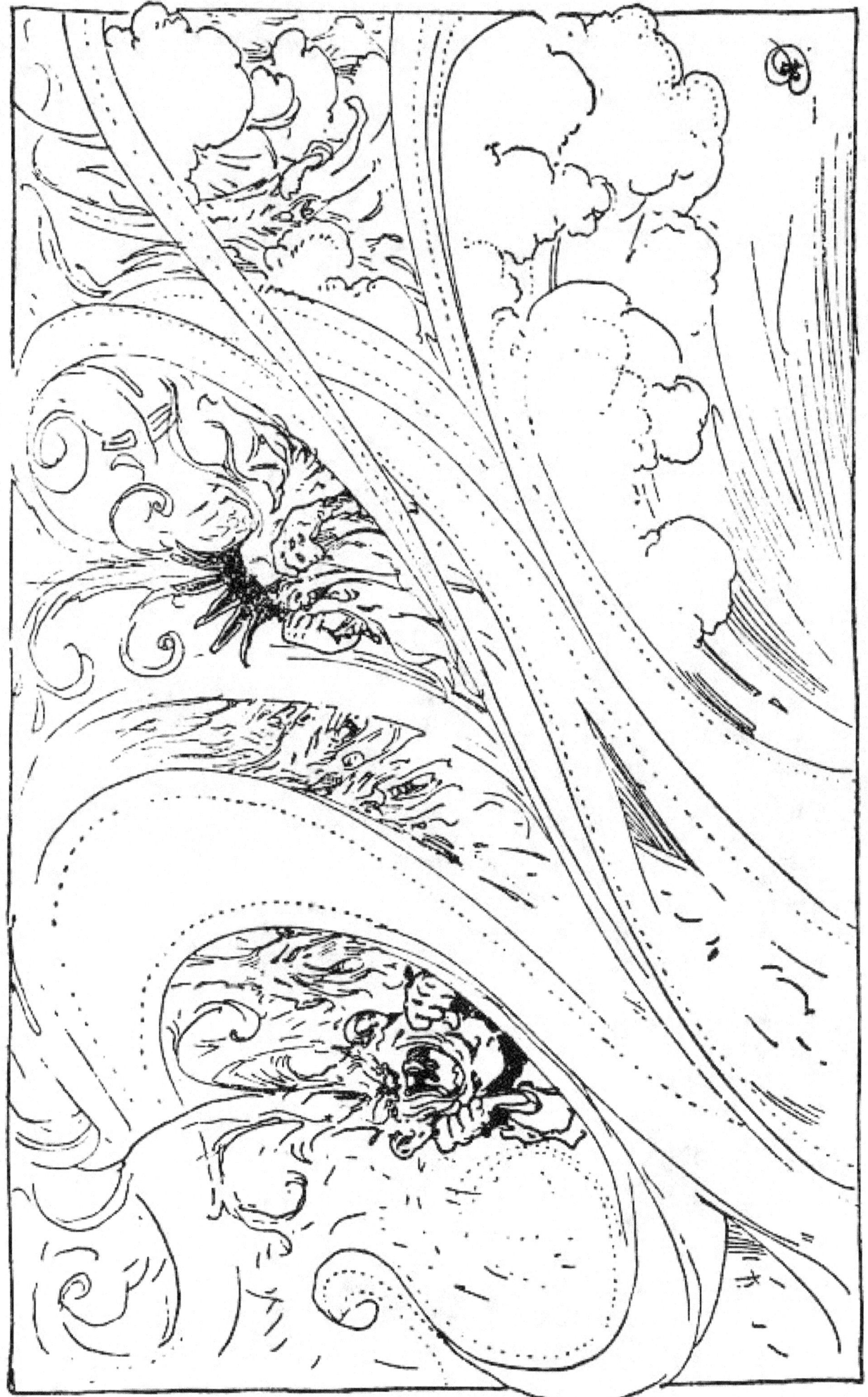

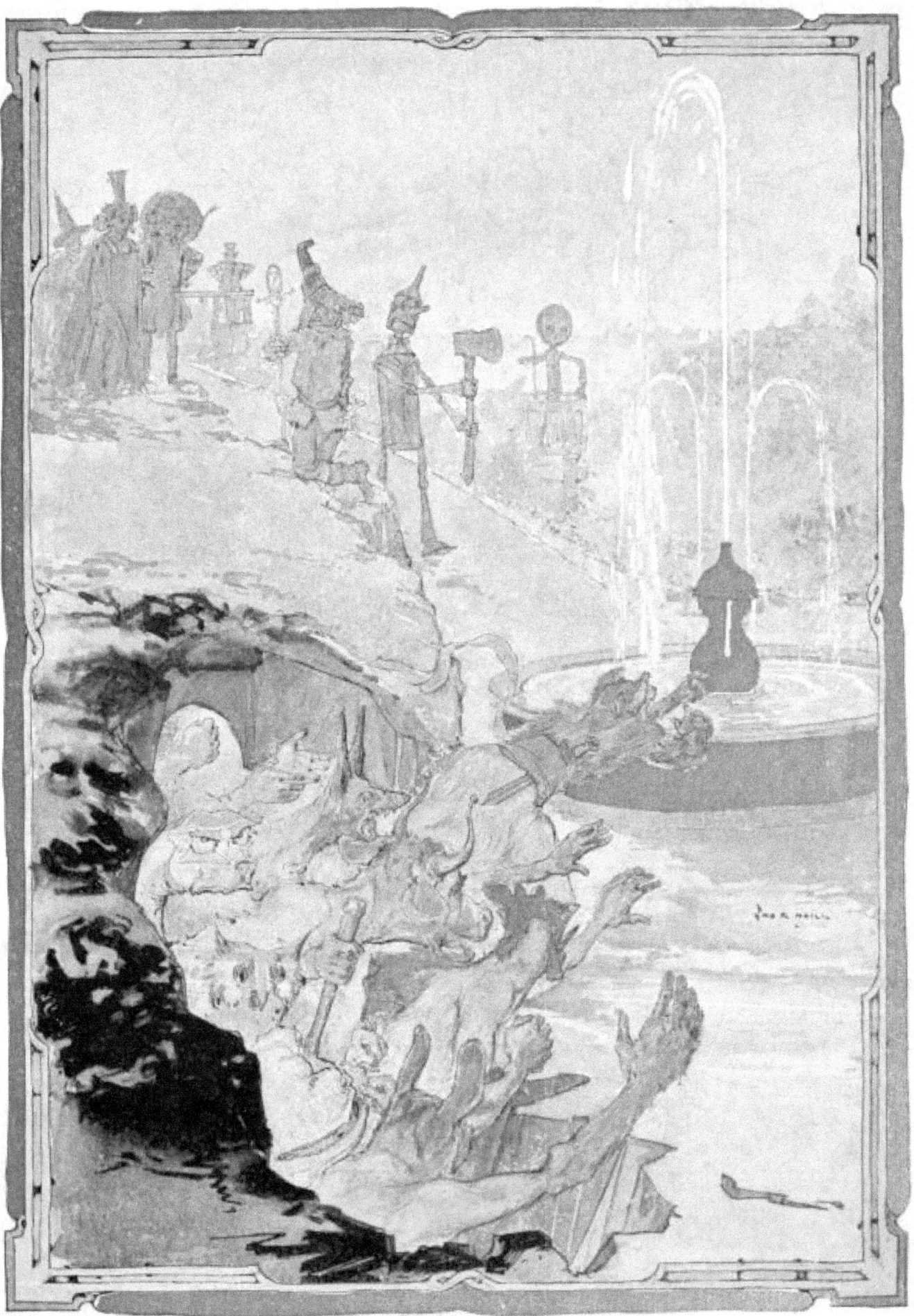

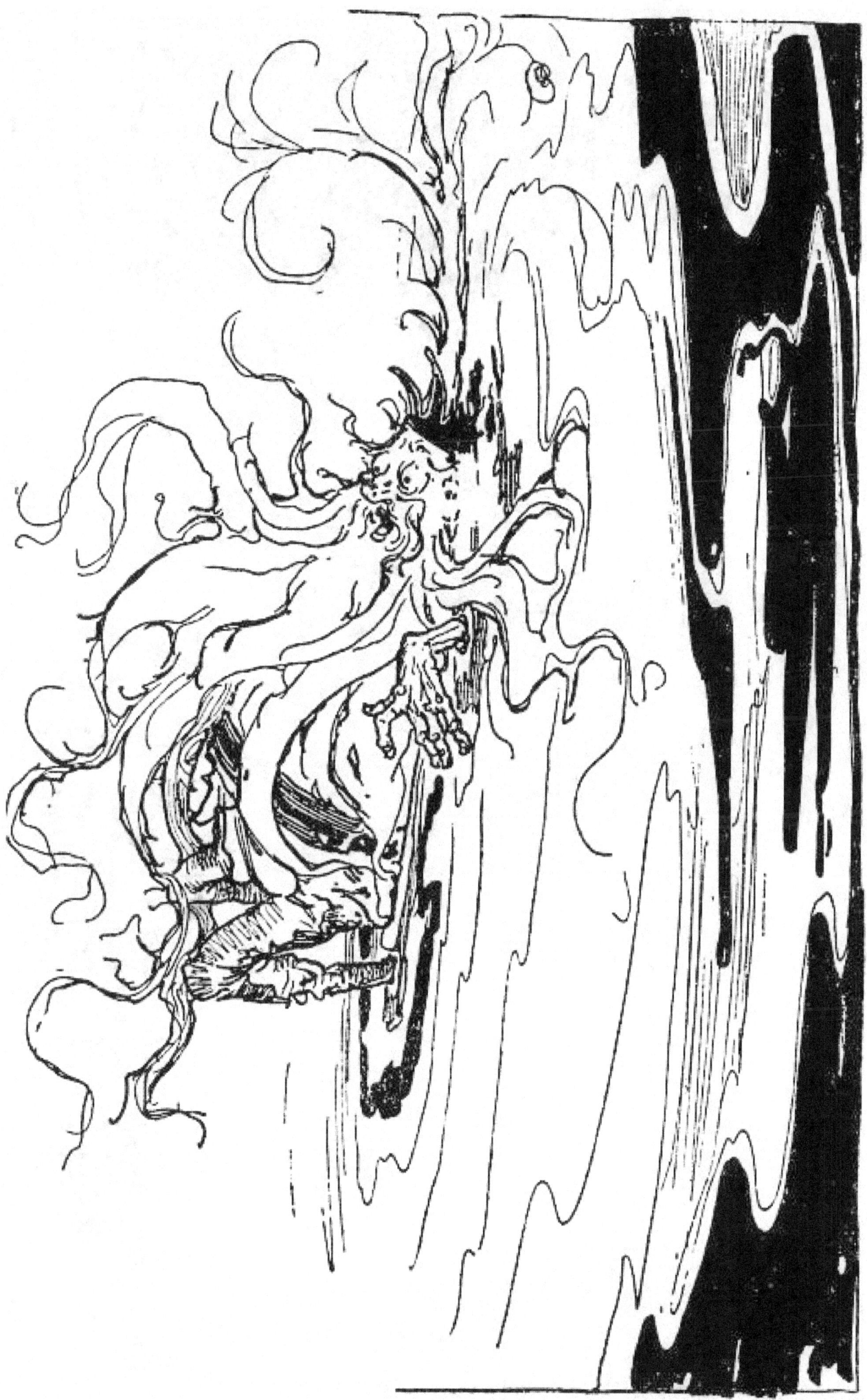

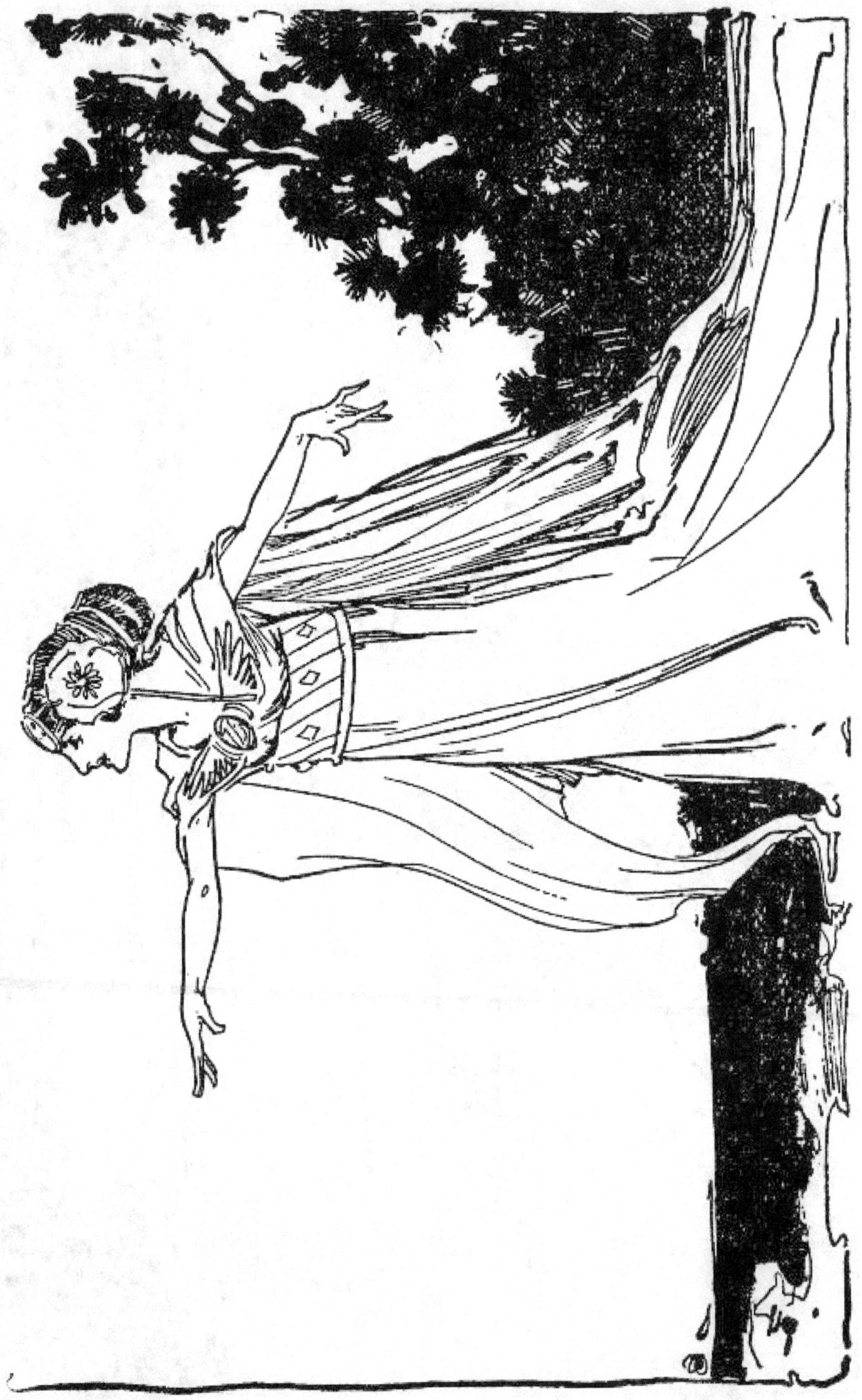

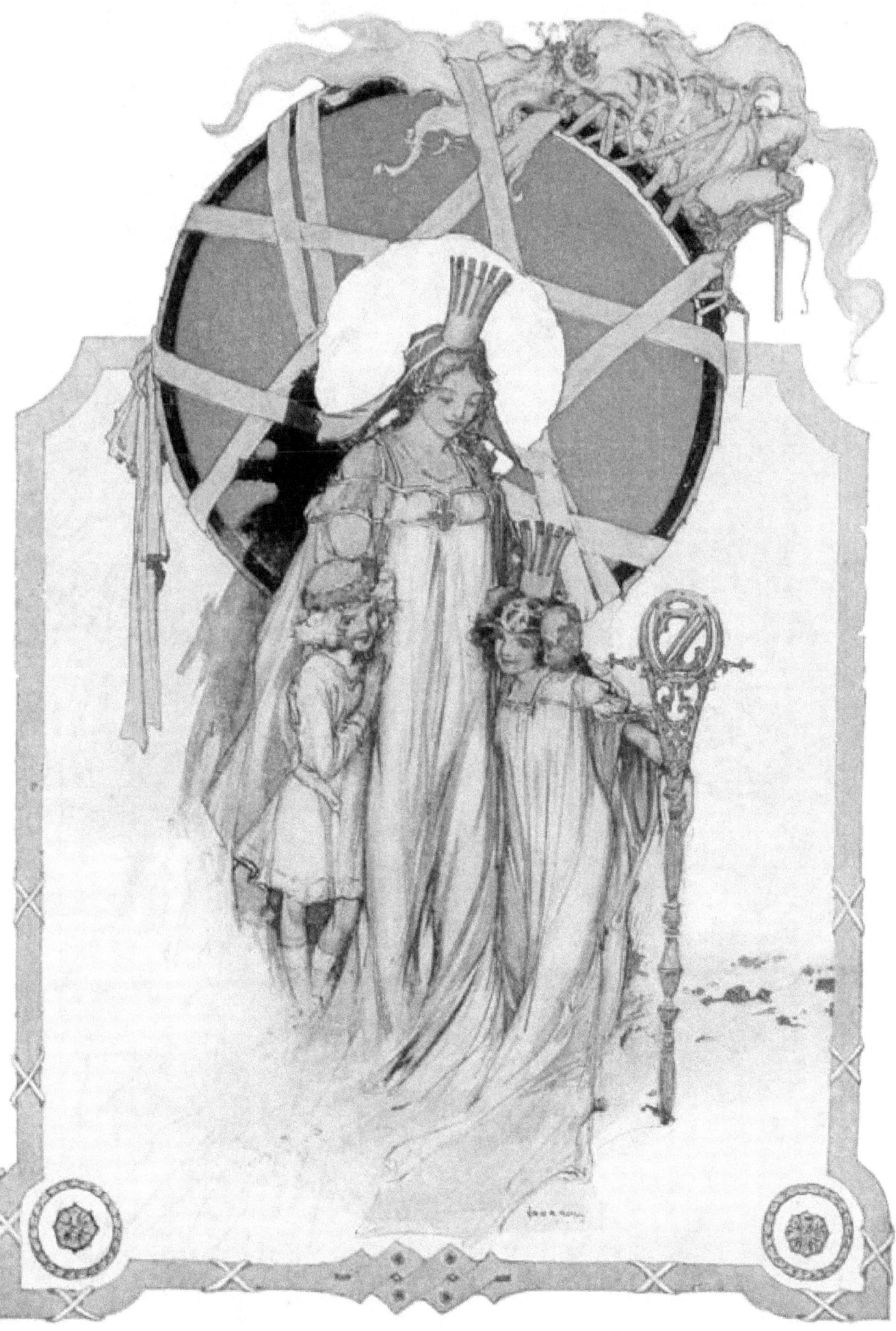

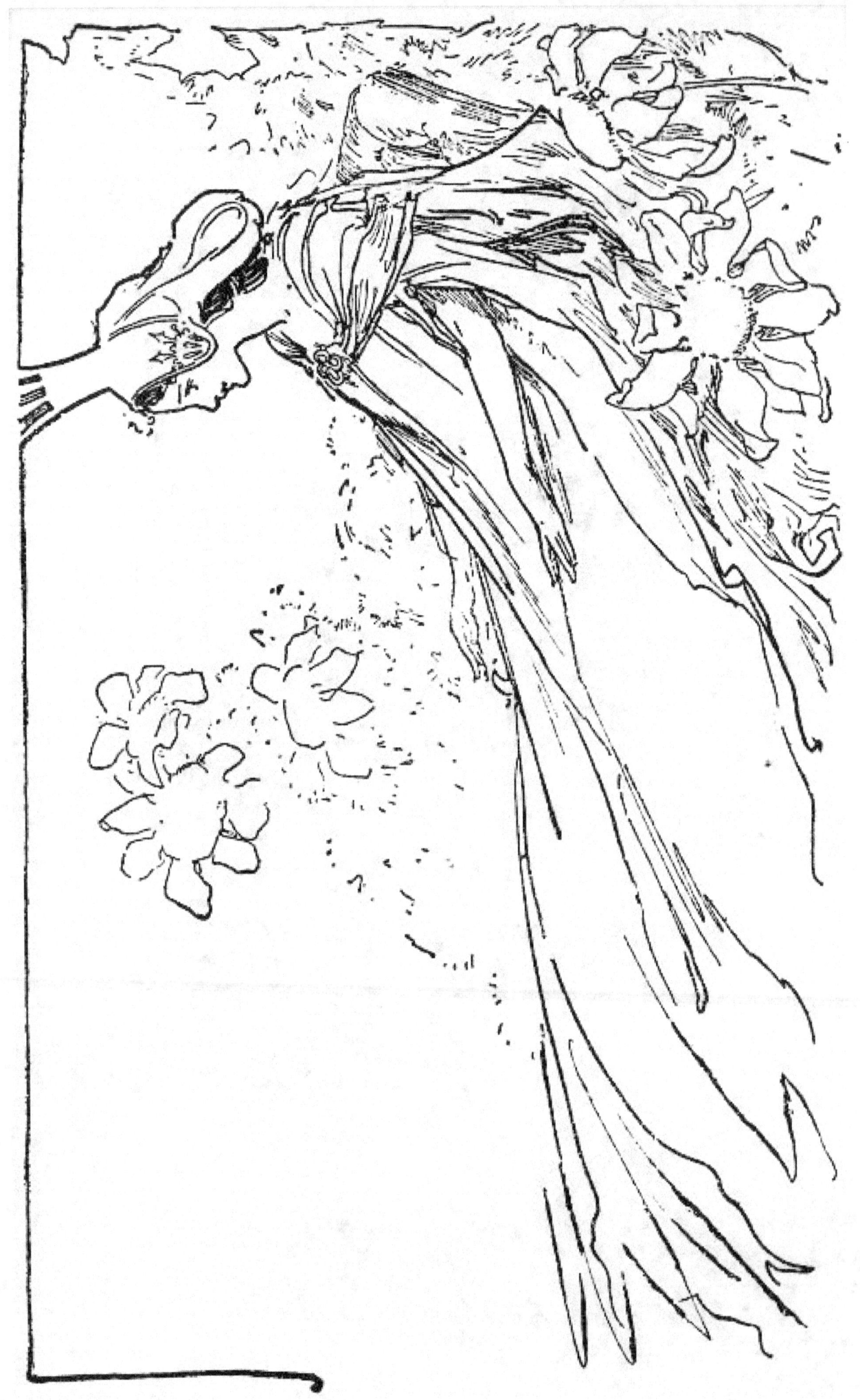

THE END

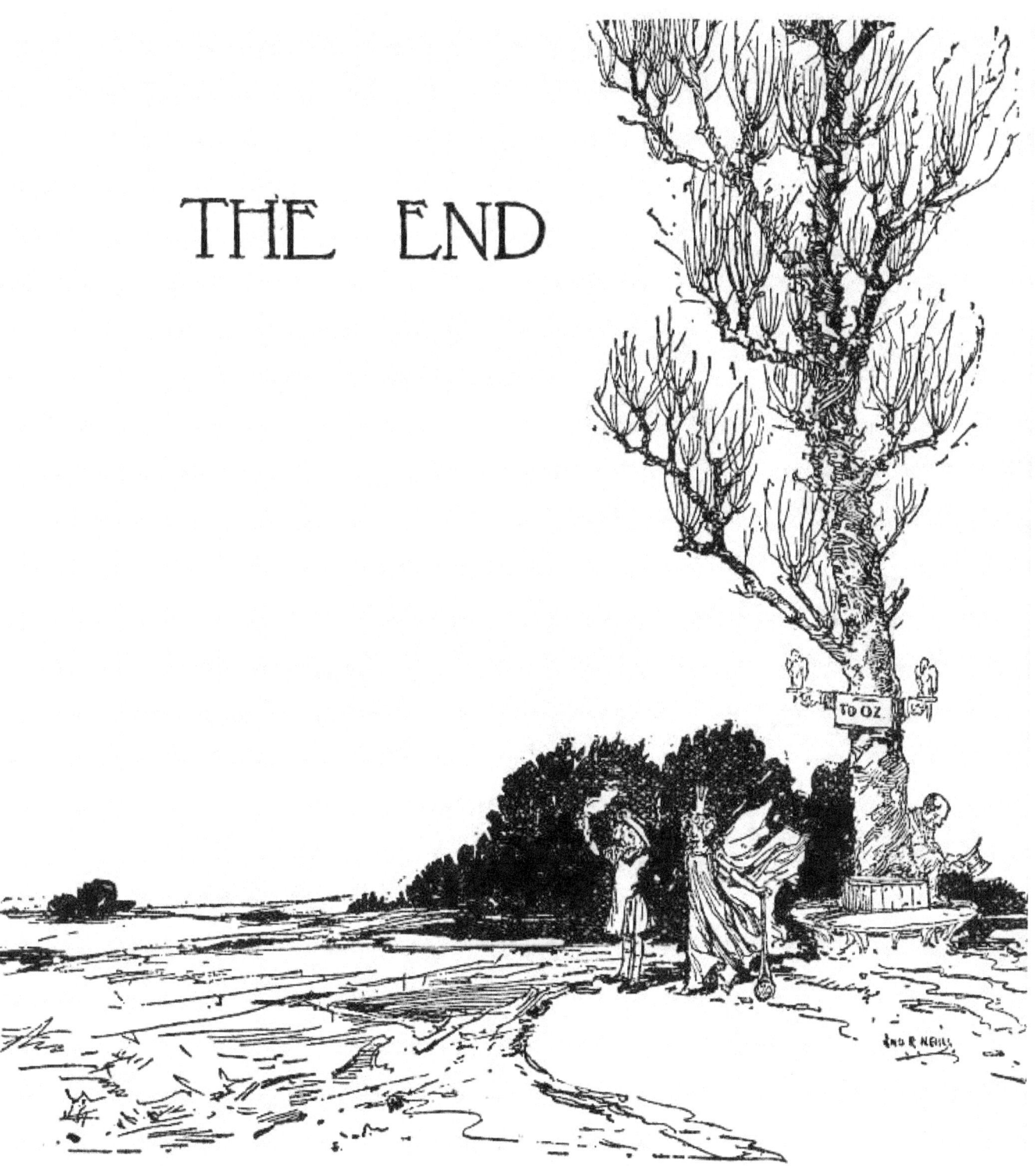